THE FINE ART OF
CALIFORNIA
INDIAN BASKETRY

THE FINE ART OF
CALIFORNIA
INDIAN BASKETRY

INTRODUCTION AND TEXT BY

BRIAN BIBBY

CROCKER ART MUSEUM

SACRAMENTO

IN ASSOCIATION WITH HEYDAY BOOKS, BERKELEY

This book is being published on the occasion of the exhibition *The Fine Art of California Indian Basketry* organized by the Crocker Art Museum, Sacramento, California. The exhibition was made possible by significant contributions from the Rockefeller Foundation; the National Endowment for the Arts, a federal agency; and the California Council for the Humanities. Additional funding was received from the Sacramento Metropolitan Arts Commission, Rumsey Band of Wintun Indians, the California Arts Council, and PG&E.

Exhibition Schedule

Crocker Art Museum	Autry Museum of Western Heritage
Sacramento, California	Los Angeles, California
August 2–November 3, 1996	March 22–June 1, 1997

Published in association with Heyday Books. Please address orders, inquiries, and correspondence to
Heyday Books
Box 9145
Berkeley, CA 94709

Publisher's Cataloging in Publication
Bibby, Brian.
      The fine art of California Indian basketry/introduction and
  text by Brian Bibby.
      p. cm.
      Includes bibliographical references.
      ISBN 0-930588-87-8
    1. Crocker Art Museum, Sacramento. 2. Indians of North America—
California—Basket making. 3. Basket-making—California—History
I. Title.

E78.C15B53 1996   746.41'2'089'97
                         QBI96-40067

Editorial and Production Coordination: Malcolm Margolin and Wendy Low
Editing: Carol Christensen and Pat Shell
Cover and Interior Design: Tracy Dean and Jack Myers, DesignSite, Berkeley
Color Separation: Canterbury Press, Berkeley
Printing and Binding: Imago (U.S.A.) Inc.

Printed in China

10 9 8 7 6 5 4

Front cover photos. Top row, left to right: Guadalupe Arenas, Basket (p.92); Amy Smoker, Woman's Ceremonial Cap (p.68); Lena Dick, Basket (p.99). Middle row: Mary, Seed Beater (p.25); Tubatulabal Gift Basket (p.84); Elizabeth Hickox, Lidded Trinket Basket (p.95). Bottom row: Pomo Gift Basket (p.80); Maria Marta, Presentation Basket (p.9); Mary Tecuyas, Cooking Basket (p.57).
Back cover photo. Carrie Bethel, Basket (p.98).

CONTENTS

FOREWORD

In February 1993 the Crocker Art Museum and the California Indian Basketweavers Association (CIBA) began exploring the possibility of developing an exhibition of California Indian baskets. While covering the cultural and historic aspects of California Indian basketweaving, we wanted especially to emphasize that these baskets were world-class works of art.

The Crocker is a most suitable venue for such an exhibition. Founded in 1885, it is the oldest public art museum in the West. Highlights of the permanent collection include old master paintings and drawings, nineteenth-century California painting, and twentieth-century art from northern California.

The Crocker Art Museum has a long-standing tradition of presenting in a fine arts context exhibitions featuring what generally have been considered craft media, including ceramics, fibers, and glass. Its California crafts shows, organized by the Creative Arts League of Sacramento, brought attention to these media and were significant in the development of the museum's outstanding ceramics collection.

Also, it is a mission of the Crocker Art Museum to explore and share the art of California. We are furthermore committed to presenting and interpreting Native American art in our region, as exemplified in our 1985 exhibition *The Extension of Tradition: Contemporary Northern California Native American Art in Cultural Perspective.* Thus, with *The Fine Art of California Indian Basketry,* we are pleased to present a survey of one of California's indigenous art forms, as practiced from the nineteenth century through modern times.

The exhibition and this publication examine the subtle differences in form and intention in California Indian basketry and help us broaden our understanding of how individual creativity may flourish within a strong formal tradition. Because we hope to focus attention on weaving as an art form, it is important that, whenever possible, we identify weavers by name. In doing so, we are especially pleased to dispel the myth that the artistic production of native cultures is necessarily anonymous. Moreover, by featuring a number of examples by artists active today, *The Fine Art of California Indian Basketry* acknowledges the continued vitality of both California Indian communities and their weaving traditions.

This exhibition and its programs represent an exciting opportunity for the Crocker Art Museum, and we are deeply appreciative of the enthusiasm and talent of the many people who have contributed to the project. We are very grateful to CIBA members, who have participated as advisors for more than three years, contributing substantially to the exhibition concept and providing assistance in identifying resources for the exhibition, publication, and related programs.

I would like to thank Brian Bibby, guest curator, for the many hours he spent contacting individuals, communities, and museums, and working with the steering committee to make the difficult selection of sixty-two baskets from a wealth of material available. In developing this publication, he has worked with scholars, collectors, and the friends and families of weavers to augment scant biographical information and offer a greater understanding of the motifs and techniques of the baskets.

Malcolm Margolin, publisher of Heyday Books, provided vision for the publication, as well as editorial sensitivity and expertise. We all benefit from his enthusiasm that this exhibition and publication be brought to a wide audience.

The exhibition and this book would not have happened without the excellent work of the Crocker's curator of art, Janice Driesbach, who coordinated the entire project. She and the other members of the Crocker Art Museum staff, including registrar Paulette Hennum, curatorial assistant Karen Martin, and curator of education KD Kurutz, skillfully managed the many details required of a major loan exhibition and extensive public programs. We are indebted to the lenders to the exhibition, who have agreed to share cherished parts of their environments so that others may benefit.

We are also very grateful for significant contributions to *The Fine Art of California Indian Basketry* from The Rockefeller Foundation; the National Endowment for the Arts, a federal agency; the California Council for the Humanities; the Sacramento Metropolitan Arts Commission; the Rumsey Band of Wintun Indians, and PG&E.

Finally, on behalf of the Crocker, we wish to thank the artists, whose weaving enriches the lives of all Californians.

Stephen C. McGough
Director

THE CALIFORNIA INDIAN BASKETWEAVERS ASSOCIATION

The California Indian Basketweavers Association (CIBA) is a native-run organization. Our main goal is "to preserve, promote and perpetuate California Indian basketweaving traditions." With this in mind, we have been pleased to work with the Crocker Art Museum on *The Fine Art of California Indian Basketweaving* publication and exhibition.

CIBA had its beginning at the first California Indian Basketweavers Gathering held at Ya-Ka-Ama, Forestville, in 1991. Native basketweavers had come together from reservations and communities throughout California to share their skills, knowledge, thoughts, and feelings on traditional basketry. The gathering brought out tears and laughter, song and dance, concerns and prayers. It brought all of us closer as a family of weavers, and we left knowing that we were not alone.

The tears at this first gathering were for the weavers before us, some of whom are featured in this publication–the "master basketweavers" who taught many of us at CIBA how to carry on the tradition. The laughter came from the wonderful stories told. Songs were shared by weavers and by our friends, the dancers, who came to honor us. The concerns were many. We especially found ourselves addressing the fact that herbicides

and pesticides that government agencies and others were spraying on our traditional gathering places were affecting many weavers. Also pressing was the fact that access to certain lands was no longer free, that many weavers felt isolated because they had no one to talk with about basketry, and that potential weavers in certain areas needed teachers to help continue their basketry tradition.

Over the years CIBA has addressed all of these issues and more. We are working with government and private landowners to end the spraying of herbicides and pesticides on our gathering grounds; we are working among ourselves to strengthen skills and resolve; and we continue, with collaborations such as this, to share our knowledge, promote understanding, and ultimately to ensure that basketry will always be a living art form of California Indian people.

For more information about the California Indian Basketweavers Association, please contact us at 16894 China Flats Rd., Nevada City, CA 95959.

Jennifer D. Bates
Chair, California Indian Basketweavers Association

PREFACE

California Indian basketry is notable for its remarkable diversity. Baskets vary from one part of the state to another, and a given community might produce a wide array of basket types. More than that, individual weavers often change and develop during the course of their life, displaying great individuality and innovation within the parameters established by long-standing traditions.

Although originally created for functional purposes, such as containers, cookware, and cradles, California Indian baskets, both historically and today, are more than just utilitarian objects. Rather, they embody aesthetic intentions and impact audiences well beyond their traditional communities. The artistic intent is evident even in the earliest basket presented in this book, the Chumash gift basket made in the first quarter of the nineteenth century *(page 9)*. Here the weaver, Maria Marta, has recorded her name on the rim of the basket, testimony to her pride of accomplishment and desire to be associated with her work, much as Western artists since the Renaissance have signed their major achievements. Further, the images of Spanish medallions woven into the body of the basket attest to the influence of outside sources on native basketry designs virtually from the onset of European contact.

The fact that California weavers, whether identified by name or only by tribal designation, have pursued aesthetic concerns is further documented by examples such as the burden baskets made in Lake, Mendocino, and Shasta Counties in the early 1890s *(pages 15, 17, and 21)*. Their varied forms, ranging from the bell-shaped Pomo example to the elegant funnel created by a Wailaki weaver, suggest that the artists were responding to more than utility: were function the weaver's sole concern, the most efficient shape for its purpose would likely have spread from one community to another.

Also, as objects designed for transport and heavy use, burden baskets clearly do not demand surface decoration to function. However, in each case, the maker has not only embellished the form, but has created elaborate and dynamic patterns with several materials. The conifer roots, bear grass, and willow shoots, each separately gathered and laboriously prepared, provide contrasting colors and reinforce the forms with which they are integrated. The monochromatic "start" of the Pomo basket appears seamlessly to become first a herringbone pattern, and then it is transformed into a band of diamonds that intersects diagonal zig-zag shapes. This pattern is at once sophisticated and technically challenging, particularly as it is realized on a surface that swells, contracts, then turns outward once again. Stunning when the basket is at rest, its visual interest was undoubtedly strengthened by the motion created when it was carried, offering a heightened dynamism and complexity. It is ironic that while early twentieth century European artists were turning toward abstraction in part as an effort to maintain the two-dimensionality of the picture plane, Native Californian weavers were using abstract motifs to reinforce the three-dimensionality of their forms.

California Indian weavers, even when introducing new elements, incorporate communal values and respond to established criteria. This is in contrast to contemporary painters and sculptors, whose contributions are customarily judged by their ability to reinvent artistic vocabularies and establish new norms. Perhaps because baskets reflect shared cultural values and experiences, the accomplishments of renowned weavers are often uncredited, at least outside their communities. Thus, outstanding examples of basketry may be identified solely by tribal origin and type—"Pomo burden basket," for example, or "Tubatulabal gift basket"—or with the name of the maker recorded only secondarily. However, study of the many works documented to named weavers, such as Elizabeth Hickox, Fanny Brown, Lena Dick, and others in both museum and private collections should allow for new understandings of their makers' distinctive styles and their importance both as individual and innovative artists and as conveyors of traditional practice to weavers active today.

In arguing that Native California basketry merits recognition and appreciation as an art form, it is critical to acknowledge the underlying aesthetic principles that communicate not only to the cultures in which they were created but beyond. Not unlike ceramics dating from ancient Greece, the Song Period in China, or modern Japan, the symmetrical shapes of most baskets enclose space, imposing order by isolating a segment of our diffuse experience. *The stability inherent in many basket forms is reinforced by design elements that acknowledge gravitational forces, while moving the eye along and across the surface. Additionally, the materials that go into Native Californian baskets offer a distinctive aesthetic experience. For example, while the sensual qualities evoked by naturally growing redbud and willow shoots, bear grass, maidenhair fern stems, and sedge roots are most powerfully felt by the weavers and their helpers, residues of their earthy origins are perceived by viewers as well. These include the smells, sounds, and tastes associated with tending, gathering, and preparing materials. Thus the natural environment from which materials are derived, as well as the handwork entailed in the splitting, soaking, and weaving processes, afford basketry a strong psychic impact among both native and non-native members of a society where contact with nature and with handformed objects have become increasingly rare. Basketry may afford a synesthetic experience to sensitive viewers not unlike that sought by European artists pursuing Symbolist and later abstract concerns during the late nineteenth and early twentieth centuries.

The sensual involvement of viewers is further strengthened by the tactile character of baskets. As containers shaped by hand, they ask to be held to be fully experienced. Even isolated under a vitrine in a museum setting, their variegated textures engage visitors. Although relatively undifferentiated in its surface, for example, the Konkow feasting basket (*page 61*) begs to be touched, with the contrasting redbud and willow shoots (and color variations within them) promising different tactile sensations. The viewer likewise is eager to rub fingers across the even coils of Lena Dick's basket (*page 99*), in part to confirm that the open design and outlined red shapes conform to its surface. Greater surface elaboration and the introduction of such diverse materials as acorn woodpecker crest feathers, valley quail top

knots, and clamshell disc beads offer even greater potential for satisfying tactile experience.

Metal cookware has, of course, long since replaced the cooking basket in the daily life of native people; and the continued production and use of winnowing trays, gift baskets, burden baskets, dance caps, and cradleboards—all requiring extensive labor in both their immediate creation and in the tending and collecting of plant materials—represents a personal choice rather than a necessity. In some cases, decisions are made to maintain (or revive) ceremonial integrity or to extend tradition to younger generations; at other times, weaving may be given impetus by market demand. In each case, however, baskets continue to be made and used in contexts in which they could be replaced by less demanding alternatives. Indeed their continued production represents an arduous option that has been pursued with deliberation, and the satisfaction they offer can be paralleled by that realized by a collector or maker of paintings or sculpture who chooses to make and/or live with original art works because of the historical resonance and personal reward they afford.

Whereas other art forms explored today have been increasingly recognized and validated in exhibitions over the past several decades, California Indian basketry has been challenged. This is due not only to the common perception of Indian basketry as "ethnic" art, perhaps more closely allied with the crafts than with "true" arts, but also because California Indian basketry has been widely seen as moribund—an activity of the past rather than a vigorous and ongoing medium of contemporary artistic expression.

The past few years, however, have witnessed heartening changes, and there is clearly a renewed appreciation for basketry as a medium of cultural and artistic expression, both within the native community and beyond. For a number of reasons, not the least of which is the work of the California Indian Basketweavers Association, California Indian basketry is enjoying renewed attention and appreciation.

Janice Driesbach
Curator of Art, Crocker Art Museum

---

*This concept and others explored in this essay derive in part from ideas presented in discussions of ceramics criticism, notably in essays by John Perreault and Jeff Perrone, published in *American Ceramics* 4 (Winter 1986):17-37.

ACKNOWLEDGMENTS

This publication and the exhibition upon which it is based have been made possible by the participation of numerous individuals, as well as by the enthusiasm and guidance of the California Indian Basketweavers Association (CIBA). We were greatly assisted throughout by a steering committee comprised of Jennifer Bates, Brian Bibby, Sara Greensfelder, Vivien Hailstone, Carla Hills, Frank LaPena, Donna Largo, L. Frank Manriquez, Sherrie Smith-Ferri, and Kathy Wallace.

The arrangement of loans from public institutions and the consideration with which museum staff assisted the exhibition curator in retrieving important information about the collections and their help during visits to the collections is sincerely appreciated: Craig Bates (Yosemite Museum, Yosemite National Park); Carey Caldwell (Oakland Museum of California); Cheri Falkenstien-Doyle (Southwest Museum); Cheryl Ferrera (Redding Museum of Art and History); Genevieve Fisher and Leah Wolf-Whitehead (Peabody Museum of Archaeology and Ethnology, Harvard University); Leslie Freund (Phoebe A. Hearst Museum of Anthropology); Katherine Hough and Kathleen Clewell (Palm Springs Desert Museum); Scott Isaacson (Lassen Volcanic National Park); Claudia Israel (Clarke Memorial Museum); Patti Johnson (U.S. Army Corps of Engineers); Shirley Kendall (Bidwell Mansion State Historic Park); Janice Klein and William Grewe-Mullins (Field Museum of Natural History); Felicia Pickering (Smithsonian Institution); Todd Ruhstaller (Haggin Museum); Elizabeth Smart, Billie Elliston, and Sandy Taugher (California State Department of Parks and Recreation); Sherrie Smith-Ferri (Grace Hudson Museum); and Elizabeth Villa (Montgomery Gallery, Pomona College).

Gratitude is also expressed to individuals who lent baskets from their collections and offered important information regarding each piece and its weaver: Craig Bates, Loren Bommelyn, Larry Dalrymple, Mr. & Mrs. Chris Ehrke, Ron Goode, Vivien Hailstone, Carl Mautz, Marshall McKay, Mr. & Mrs. Herb Puffer, Mr. & Mrs. Gene Quintana, Eva Slater, Lori Smith, and Sherrie Smith-Ferri. Several individuals were also extremely helpful in supplying information about the weavers and securing photographs for this publication, including Dugan Aguilar, Dot Brovarney, Marvin Cohodas, Lillian Hostler, Christine Ipiña, Helen Jose, Hank Meals, Victoria Patterson, and Dorothea Theodoratus.

Throughout the planning of this exhibition several individuals have been called upon for expertise and advice of which they gave freely. The assistance of Craig Bates, Vivien Hailstone, Judith Polanich, Sherrie Smith-Ferri, and Kathy Wallace was essential in gathering information about weavers and in helping to make decisions regarding the selection of pieces.

This publication owes much to the editing skills of Carol Christensen and Pat Shell; the production and editorial assistance of Wendy Low; the design skills of Tracy Dean and Jack Myers; the color separation and production magic of Canterbury Press; and the cooperation of Snow Lion Graphics in adhering to a tight schedule.

Finally, neither the exhibition nor this publication would have been possible without significant contributions from the Rockefeller Foundation; the National Endowment for the Arts, a federal agency; the California Council for the Humanities; the Sacramento Metropolitan Arts Commission; the Rumsey Band of Wintun Indians; the California Arts Council; PG&E; Barbara Jeanne Hansen; Carla Hills; and Frank R. LaPena. We are deeply grateful for their support.

PHOTO CREDITS

In producing this publication, the Crocker Art Museum requested the highest quality color transparencies possible. We wish to acknowledge the skill and care of the following photographers.

Don Brewer (p. 73), Phillip Dresser (p. 60), James Hart (p. 109), F. L. Hizer (p. 51), Tom Liden (p. 45, 94, 105, 108), Lowell Martinson (p. 21, 102, 103), Gene Prince (p. 9, 66), Schenk and Schenk Photography (p. 91, 93), Ron Schwager (p. 61), Veronica Tagland (p. 77), Robert Woolard (p. 25, 36, 38, 97), Don Yee (p. 17, 27, 33, 34, 35, 39, 44, 56, 58, 59, 68, 70, 78, 79, 81, 83, 85, 95, 98, 99, 101)

NATIVE CALIFORNIA

Map adapted from *The Way We Lived: California Indian Stories, Songs, and Reminiscences* edited by Malcolm Margolin. © 1993. Used with permission of Heyday Books.

    This map gives a simplified picture of Native California. The term "Pomo," for example, covers some seventy politically independent groups who speak seven related but mutually unintelligible languages. "Miwok" likewise covers several different groups, and in the text that follows might be spelled "Mewuk" or "Miwuk" depending on local preference.

CONTRIBUTORS

In the pages that follow, each basket is introduced with a commentary by Brian Bibby, guest curator of *The Fine Art of California Indian Basketweaving* exhibition. Much of the additional commentary was elicited at a colloquium held at the Crocker Art Museum on January 22, 1996, funded in part by a special grant from the California Council for the Humanities. Native basketweavers, native artists in other media, and a number of scholars assembled to review slides of the baskets and engage in a lively dialogue about the techniques, aesthetics, and social history of each basket. Those who attended the colloquium included Craig Bates, Jennifer Bates, Brian Bibby, Denise Davis, Vivien Hailstone, Jean LaMarr, Frank LaPena, Donna Largo, L. Frank Manriquez, Judith Polanich, Sherrie Smith-Ferri, Brian Tripp, Frank Tuttle, and Kathy Wallace.

Although they were not able to attend the colloquium, additional comments were solicited from Bruce Bernstein, Harry Fonseca, and Lori Smith. Comments by Bette Holmes and Kathleen Smith were drawn from the documentary videotape *Pomo Basketweavers: A Tribute to Three Elders* written by Beverly R. Ortiz and produced by David Ludwig, Creative Light Productions.

We are extremely grateful to all for giving so generously of their time and knowledge.

Craig Bates, curator of ethnography, Yosemite National Park, is co-author of *Tradition and Innovation: A Basket History of the Indians of the Yosemite-Mono Lake Area,* and one of the leading authorities on California Indian basketry.

Jennifer Bates (Northern Mewuk) is tribal administrator for the Tuolumne Band of Mewuk Indians, traditional basketweaver, and chairperson of the California Indian Basketweavers Association.

Bruce Bernstein is the director of the Museum of Indian Arts and Culture/Laboratory of Anthropology in Santa Fe, New Mexico. He has a Ph.D. in anthropology from the University of New Mexico, has been a longtime student of California Indian basketry traditions, and has authored numerous articles on the subject.

Brian Bibby is an independent scholar who has worked for over twenty-five years with elders of many of the Central Valley and foothill communities. A highly regarded expert in the song, dance, language, and artistic traditions of Native California, he has taught at a number of institutions and has served as consultant and guest curator for many cultural and folk arts programs in California.

Denise Davis (Maidu) learned weaving from Maidu elder Lilly Baker and Pomo/Patwin weaver Mabel McKay. Davis has exhibited her work and demonstrated basketmaking throughout California and the western United States. She is also an artist whose mixed media works often employ basketry design motifs.

Harry Fonseca (Maidu) is a nationally recognized artist whose paintings and prints are inspired by the Maidu creation story, the mythic trickster figure Coyote, traditional native dance, and Maidu basketry. Recent works draw from pictograph images found throughout the West.

Vivien Hailstone (Yurok/Karuk, and member of the Hupa Tribe) is a veteran teacher of traditional Yurok/Karuk basketry and has been instrumental in efforts to perpetuate these traditions throughout northern California.

Bette Holmes (Dry Creek Pomo/Healdsburg Pomo/ Wappo) is the grandniece of the late Pomo/Wappo master weaver Laura Somersal, and spent much of her childhood living with her near Healdsburg. She is a major contributor to the section of the *Pomo Basketweavers* videotape which featured Mrs. Somersal. Mrs. Holmes lives in Pleasanton, California.

Jean LaMarr (Paiute/Pit River) is one of the leading contemporary native artists in the country. Her works have appeared in numerous one-person and group shows. She has taught at the Institute of American Indian Arts in Santa Fe, and recently offered workshops in printmaking at her studio in Susanville. LaMarr is well known as a muralist and has often involved native youth as contributing artists in her murals.

Frank LaPena (Wintu) is professor of art and director of Native American studies at California State University, Sacramento. He has served as a curatorial consultant for the National Museum of the American Indian, Smithsonian Institution. As an artist, he has had his paintings, prints, and sculptures featured in numerous one-person and group exhibitions.

Donna Largo (Cahuilla) began collecting materials and weaving baskets under the tutelage of her grandmother, and later received a California Arts Council master/apprentice grant to work with master Cahuilla weaver Rosalie Valencia. Largo is a teacher and has been active in demonstrating and speaking on weaving at gatherings and symposia in southern California.

L. Frank Manriquez (Tongva/Ajachme) is a basketweaver, printmaker, writer, and illustrator whose work has been featured in numerous exhibitions and publications. A member of the board of the California Indian Basketweavers Association, Manriquez has studied Native Californian baskets in European museums and is knowledgeable about environmental issues that impact weavers.

Judith Polanich, senior project ethnologist, NAGPRA Unit, at the Phoebe A. Hearst Museum of Anthropology (UC Berkeley), has served as visiting curator and consultant to the Los Angeles County Museum of Natural History Native American Hall, the Mendocino County Museum Elsie Allen collection, and the Fresno Metropolitan Museum "Strands of Time" exhibition.

Kathleen Smith (Dry Creek Pomo/Bodega Miwok) is an artist and writer. She was a student of Pomo/Wappo weaver Laura Somersal as well as of her mother, Lucy Smith, and worked with both on the Warm Springs Dam Project as the coordinator of the Native American Advisory Committee for the WSDP Cultural Resources Study.

Lori Smith (Yurok/Wailaki) is a weaver living in Ferndale. She is a trustee of the Spinas/Brown Basketry Collection at the College of the Redwoods in Eureka where she is also pursuing a degree in medical assistance.

Sherrie Smith-Ferri (Dry Creek Pomo/Bodega Miwok) is a Ph.D. candidate in sociocultural anthropology at the University of Washington (Seattle) and curator at the Grace Hudson Museum in Ukiah. Smith-Ferri has published and addressed symposia regarding the history of Pomo weavers and basketry.

Brian Tripp (Karuk) is a leading contemporary artist in California, has exhibited in major galleries and museums, and received a Headlands Center for the Arts Fellowship. Tripp has utilized the geometric design tradition found in Karuk basketry in much of his art over the past twenty-five years. He is also a fine traditional Karuk singer.

Frank Tuttle (Yuki/Wailaki/Konkow) is a well-known artist whose work includes realistic representations and abstracted impressions of traditional Native Californian cultures. Tuttle is an accomplished basketweaver who specializes in traditional men's stick baskets such as cradles. He is also a schoolteacher.

Kathy Wallace (Hupa/Yurok/Karuk) is a basketweaver and has spoken on and demonstrated traditional basketweaving throughout California. Wallace teaches weaving classes, co-founded the California Indian Basketweavers Association, and has served as co-curator and consultant to museums in northern California.

INTRODUCTION

Before the coming of Europeans, indigenous California was one of the most culturally diverse regions of the world. Some 500 autonomous communities speaking as many as 80 mutually unintelligible languages made their homes throughout the varied landscapes of the region. Numbering an estimated 350,000 people, they achieved perhaps the greatest population density in North America outside of Mexico and maintained stable and successful ways of living over a long period of time in a wide variety of habitats.

While archaeological evidence from sites such as Borax Lake (Lake County) documents human activity in California at roughly 11,000 years ago, native oral literatures tell of the creation of people at specific places in the landscape outside the logic of quantified time. As Konkow elder Henry Azbill would explain, "We just say a long time ago." Either way, it is clear that the presence of native people in California has tremendous depth and complexity, and extended over all the diverse environments that comprise California.

In many ways the state's native basketry traditions mirror this complexity and diversity. Native Californian baskets might be initially viewed as inventions to solve problems. First and foremost, baskets were needed. They were, for example, necessary for gathering, processing, cooking, eating, and storing a variety of foods. As basketry scholar Bruce Bernstein recently noted: "Baskets were integral to the activities that were the foundations of life—infants were carried in baskets, meals were prepared in baskets, and baskets were given as gifts to mark an individual's entrance into and exit from this world."

Yet even when the needs for a basket were similar, baskets nevertheless varied depending on the traditions of the people making them. Thus, for instance, a Pomo burden basket is quite different from a Luiseño burden basket in weaving techniques, materials, shape, design layout schemes and placement,

Rumsien Ohlone woman of Monterey illustrated by José Cordero, 1791. Courtesy of The Smithsonian Institution, Washington.

and perhaps even in the particular way it is designed to be used.

Throughout California the relationship between baskets and acorns was an intimate one, with up to eight different baskets figuring into the gathering, processing, cooking, and eating of acorns—certainly the most significant food staple of the region. While certain species of oaks provided acorns that were preferable to others, by and large any of ten or more oak species were harvested by Native Californians. In addition to being available and abundant, at least during good years, acorns could also be stored fairly well for future use without spoiling.

Acorns, however, are inedible in their natural state and require a specific method of processing. First the shell must be cracked open and the meat extracted and dried. Then it must be pounded with a stone pestle in a stone (or wooden) mortar, sometimes fitted with a hopper basket. The resulting flour is then sifted on the surface of a basketry tray: the fine particles lodge within the crevices of the weave while the coarse granules roll off the edge of the tray to be repounded.

The finely pounded flour is then tapped out of the sifting basket into a specially prepared sand basin, where water is poured over it to leach out the bitter tannin. When the tannin is removed, the dough is gathered and any sand residue is washed from the bottom layer. The dough is placed in a cooking basket, mixed with water, and cooked by introducing red-hot stones to the mixture. These stones are stirred about, new stones added when the first cool, until the liquid boils. Soon a thick soup is fully cooked and quite edible.

This revolutionary process, which may have appeared between 5,000 and 6,000 years ago in California, is an example of the intelligence, skill, and adaptability of these early people to their environment. There is a popular notion that "hunting and gathering people" simply walked about without much forethought, gathering edible foods at will. In reality, the knowledge and skills required for life within that framework are much more sophisticated than most people realize.

Two other basket types that have a nearly universal distribution throughout California are the burden basket—generally a conically shaped, twined basket—and the scoop-like seed beater. These two baskets were often used together to harvest grass seeds. The seeds were generally gathered by whacking the seed clusters with a woven seed beater, knocking them into the wide, open mouth of a burden basket. The seeds were usually winnowed in a basketry tray and then tossed together with a hot coal to be parched or toasted. They were eaten either dry or in a porridge popularly known to pioneer Californians as *pinole*. The process of parching was noted with admiration by the French explorer Jean François de La Pérouse who visited Monterey in 1786:

Konkow woman stone-boiling acorn soup. Photo taken at Foreman Ranch near Bidwell Bar by John Hudson, 1903. Courtesy of The Field Museum of Natural History, Chicago.

> The whole art of this cookery consists in roasting the grain before it is reduced to meal. As the Indian women have no clay pottery or metallic vessels for this operation, they perform it in baskets of bark by using small burning wood coals. They turn these vessels with such dexterity and rapidity that they succeed in causing the grain to swell and burst without burning the basket, though made of combustible material. (We can affirm that our best coffee is far from being roasted with equal skill.)

In addition to their use in the food quest, baskets were an integral part of people's lives in other ways. Throughout much of the region caps were made. These were worn primarily by women, although among some northwestern California groups men also wore caps. The Yurok, Karuk, Tolowa, Wiyot, and Hupa recognized two basic styles of caps: a work cap, which usually included a minimal amount of overlay design work, and a dress or ceremonial cap that was richly overlaid.

Baby cradles were made throughout the region and appear in two basic forms: a sitting cradle and a flat-backed cradle with a hood or sunshade. Some baskets were made solely for ceremonial purposes, such as the Jump Dance basket of the Klamath-Trinity River region. Even basically practical basket types with day-to-day use, such as a cooking basket or a soup basket, might be found within a ceremonial context. It was a tradition among the Nomlaki and Patwin, for example, to hold a "sing" in which a series of acorn songs were performed as a prayer for the upcoming crop. Singers held a cooking basket in an inverted position and gently patted the basket's base to keep rhythm. During a climactic moment of the Brush Dance performed in north-western California, two dancers—one male and one female—hold small soup baskets in their hands while they dance: a basket so used is generally referred to as a "medicine basket." At a Pomo wedding, a large twined storage basket adorned with clam-shell disc beads and quail plumes is offered as payment and an exchange of property from one family to another. People are buried with baskets, and in former times baskets were made to be burned at annual memorial ceremonies.

Basketry in California thus spilled out over the bounds of necessity into other aspects of people's social and ceremonial lives. Indeed, the extreme integrity of the basketweaving techniques and the beauty of shape and design make it clear that native weavers "developed the craft of basket manufacture beyond the requirements of successful utilitarian function," and that baskets "were an ever-present source of aesthetic pleasure and visual enrichment in the context of everyday life." For the individual, as an artist within the community, "baskets were a medium for the expression of talent and artistic sensibility, prestige and pride" (McLendon and Holland 1979:104).

Tribal oral traditions often attribute the original knowledge of basketry to mythic or spiritual sources. Such myths are not simply naive stories that try to explain how baskets came about, but rather are highly meaningful oral texts illustrating the integral role of basketry in the lives of people and their relationships to the larger world around them. "Baskets were not given in creation, but rather, they were part of the creation." (Bernstein 1996:7)

The basketry of Native California may be without equal among the world cultures in terms of technological excellence, extent of types developed for use, artistic development, and consistent quality throughout most of the region. A wide variety of basket-making technologies are found within California—six distinct twining techniques (plain, diagonal, three strand, three strand braid, wrapped, and lattice) and three major coiling methods (single rod, three rod, and soft bundle). Wicker work also appeared among some groups for construction of seed-harvesting baskets.

Moreover, the particular traditions followed in executing any of these technologies often varied significantly from one group to another. Technological features such as the pitch of the weave in twining, the direction in which coiling proceeds (to the left or to the right), which side of the basket becomes the work surface, how materials are added, spliced, and terminated, or the particular nature of a basket's starting knot, are among many features that constitute a given weaving tradition. Indeed, there were scores of unique traditions.

Archaeological evidence suggests that twining is the older of the two techniques in California. Coiling began to appear approximately 3,000 years ago and eventually established itself throughout two-thirds of the state, the northern third of the region remaining exclusively a twining area. Most groups that adopted a coiling technique continued to twine certain types of baskets.

As has been well documented elsewhere, the impact of Ibero- and Euro-American migration into California, the subsequent episodes of genocide, the rapid displacement of native peoples, and the degradation of environment and ecosystems

Nisenan woman collecting seeds with a seed beater and burden basket, c. 1900. Courtesy of The Field Museum of Natural History, Chicago.

as a result of mining, logging, ranching, and agriculture had many serious effects on native populations and cultures. The very survival of native people in this state was once in doubt, the continuance of traditional culture even more so. By 1890 the estimated native population in California had shrunk from a third of a million people to about twenty thousand.

In many areas of the state the changes brought about by the invasion of non-Indians required new strategies for living. Within a fairly short period, a society based on hunting and gathering could no longer be maintained. Many native people found the only economy left to them was working for non-Indians as miners, ranch hands, and domestics.

How did basketry fit into this new era? Interestingly enough, traditional baskets often found use in these new forms of work. Historic drawings dating from the early 1850s illustrate winnowing baskets being used to pan gold in the mother lode. Pomoan people used their large twined storage baskets to haul hops in the fields. Konkow women carried the bricks for John Bidwell's home in their burden baskets.

But perhaps the greatest use of baskets, and a significant impetus for continuing to weave, was for the collectors' market that blossomed during the 1890s and continued to flourish into the 1930s. Native women throughout the state produced some of the finest basketry ever made during this period. Continuing to use traditional native materials and technologies, many women created new forms and began innovating with newly developed design schemes.

A tradition of adaptiveness served these women well, and they became important contributors to the household economy through their basketry. In fact, they became very important contributors. As Pomo art historian and anthropologist Sherrie Smith-Ferri noted: "The commercial basket market provided weavers and their families with a significant source of income at a time when few other means of support were available to Pomo women. Thanks to her basketweaving, Joseppa [Dick] was well-to-do by the standards of the rancheria and the local rural white community." (Smith-Ferri, 1993:62).

There were many other women across the state with reputations for their weaving. Some, like Washo weaver Datsolalee (Louisa Keyser), were regularly commissioned by dealers such as Abe Cohen, who sold her works through his Emporium Store at Lake Tahoe. During this period we begin to see more and more baskets which are made, bought, and sold as works of art. The intent or emphasis on function was becoming much less common, although there still were weavers who continued to make traditional forms over and over again. Events such as Indian Field Days in Yosemite held basketmaking competitions with cash prizes. Wealthy regulars to Yosemite, such as James Schwabacher, became important patrons to Yosemite and Mono Lake weavers such as Lucy Telles and Carrie Bethel.

Suzie and Sadie McGowan (Mono Lake Paiute) in Yosemite Valley, c. 1901. Photo by J.T. Boysen. Courtesy of National Park Service, Yosemite National Park.

By the 1940s the market for basketry began to ebb, and the Second World War brought further disruptions. Large numbers of native men left their communities for the armed services, and at the conclusion of the war numerous families, taking the new skills acquired while in the service, relocated to cities where jobs awaited as part of the post-war economy. Many of the master weavers of the early twentieth century died during this period, and few young women saw weaving as access to mainstream American culture and its economic benefits. For many young women it wasn't very chic to be an "Indian" basketweaver in the 1940s or 1950s.

However, there are always a few individuals who continue to find value in older traditions. In some culturally conservative families weaving was maintained. And it has been these individuals who have carried weaving traditions from their mothers and grandmothers, active in the nineteenth century, to the

present generation of aspiring weavers. We think of them as a "bridge" generation. Weavers such as Mabel McKay, Laura Somersal, and Ella Johnson were able to keep their traditions alive long enough for a new generation to find value in them.

By the 1960s some communities were consciously making efforts to maintain and re-energize their weaving traditions. Yurok/Karuk elder, Vivien Hailstone, recalled her efforts to organize classes in traditional weaving in Hoopa Valley with Yurok weaver Ella Johnson serving as a master teacher. Later, Vivien asked College of the Redwoods to sponsor a weaving class through it's extension program. At that time college officials, as Vivien recalled, "laughed in our faces."

Today a renaissance of weaving activity is taking place. Since its inception in 1992, the California Indian Basketweavers Association (CIBA) has made progress in motivating individuals and communities, organizing workshops, and networking among weavers. CIBA has worked to create better access to materials on public and private lands, and to oppose pesticide spraying in areas where weavers gather materials. A growing number of highly motivated, dedicated young women are now taking their respective basketry traditions into the twenty-first century, something many people, native and non-native alike, probably thought would not happen.

There are a number of important issues that confront today's weavers. Access to materials remains a nagging problem. Since the land bases of reservations and rancherias are generally too small to supply enough natural materials, getting to the right spot for the right material at the right time often means trespassing on private, corporate, county, state, or federal lands. Vivien Hailstone recalls how some weavers used to gather woodwardia ferns in Hoopa Valley early on Sunday mornings, because they knew that the local highway patrol officer was in church at that time. Several community weaving traditions may have been lost due to difficulty in obtaining weaving materials.

With certain areas inaccessible, another pressing issue arises: the quality of materials. A greatly overlooked aspect of basketmaking in California is the land "management" practices of traditional weavers. Their extensive knowledge of plants and their unique qualities, along with a long experiential relationship with plant communities, led people to maintain microenvironments which fostered healthy growing and living conditions for the plants and optimum quality materials for the weavers. By digging in certain places for generations, for example, the ground was broken up and loosened, providing optimum conditions for roots and rhizomes to grow long and straight. Coppicing of shrubs such as redbud resulted in straight, supple new growth shoots with minimum tapering. Burning produced healthy patches of bear grass, deer grass, and supple new shoots on hazel bushes. Burning also apparently helped minimize insect infestation of certain materials. The extent to which native people managed this environment has been explored by many scholars, especially Kat Anderson. (See, for example, Blackburn and Anderson, 1993).

Bald Rock Jim (Konkow) standing before items about to be burned at a mourning ceremony near Mooretown, c. 1905. Photo by S.A. Barrett. Courtesy of The American Museum of Natural History, New York.

Through the efforts of CIBA, various individuals, and tribal organizations, some headway has been made in negotiating access and instituting new policies concerning native needs for burning. Within the past three years the U.S. Forest Service has assisted in burning an area on the lower Klamath River for the creation of more favorable hazel bush conditions. Progress has been made, but problems remain. The U.S. Forest Service, for example, has recently turned down repeated requests for a moratorium on the aerial spraying of pesticides in the area of a Tuolumne County forest fire in 1993.

From the weavers' view, what makes Native California basketry one of the world's great textile traditions is the quality and properties of the materials. In addition to the aesthetic qualities of baskets and the ingenuity of their functional design, proper materials are essential for the incredible integrity of their construction. These baskets are very strong, durable works that can withstand significant weight, heat, moisture, and stress. This is due not only to sound weaving techniques, but also to the wonderful array of natural materials found in the various bio-regions of California, whose physical properties allow for such substantial and beautiful creations.

The creation of a basket from natural, hand-gathered materials is an amazing process, and the result is not lost on the weavers themselves. As Vivien Hailstone remarked, "You walk into the forest and you come out with a basket." Perhaps it is our present disassociation from all things natural, as objects made from synthetic materials seem to dominate modern life, that the wonder of knowing that someone can walk into the forest and come out with a basket is now quite remarkable.

Among the sixty-two baskets included in *Fine Art of California Indian Basketry* there are weaving materials from some twenty-nine different plants, shrubs, and trees, plus two additional items of flora used for dye and other items made of shell and feathers. With several plants, more than one part is used, and the same plant species may be harvested at different seasons for varying color or tone. In general, most weaving materials come from the roots and rhizomes of plants and trees, from the stems of certain ferns, from grass stalks, and from shoots of a variety of shrubs and trees. In all, over forty different plant species were used within California as either warp, weft, or overlay elements, or as a dye.

There are certain types of baskets that are still being made for native use. Cradles are made on a fairly regular basis in

Western Mono, Yokuts, Washo, Paiute, Yurok, Karuk, Hupa, Tolowa, and Pomo communities. Throughout much of the century, ceremonial caps have been made in the Klamath-Trinity River region for use in Brush Dances. They may in fact be in greater demand now than they were thirty years ago.

The power of the basketry tradition—its presence in day-to-day living, the reliance of people upon it, the beauty of its technology, the boldness, subtlety, and excitement of its design traditions—all have had a profound and lasting impact on native people. For many women and men, involvement in the basketry tradition has been a personal and spiritually transforming experience. It requires an intimate, reciprocal relationship with the plant

Pomo woman weaving an enormous close twine basket. Date and photographer unknown. Courtesy of The American Museum of Natural History, New York

communities. And the process of learning is still an intimate, immediate experience from master weaver to student, a method that has remained largely the same over thousands of years. For some, basketmaking has become one of the few remaining avenues to rediscovering a cultural heritage. For others, basketweaving is something your mother did, your grandmother did, and your great-grandmother did. Even for people who never lived at a time when baskets were needed to collect and process foods on a daily basis—in fact even for people who have never made a basket—basketry is a part of one's identity, as Pomo, or Karuk, or Mono.

Today baskets and their design motifs have become icons found on everything from tribal government stationery to individual business cards, T-shirts, baseball caps, silverwork, ceramics, and contemporary art. Several of California's leading native artists have been influenced significantly by the design traditions of basketry from their respective communities. These include Harry Fonseca, Frank LaPena, Frank Tuttle, Jean LaMarr, Denise Davis, David Ipiña, George Blake, and Brian Tripp. Regarding the sophistication of the design tradition in

Karuk basketry as a fundamental basis for his own work in dealing with abstract forms, Karuk artist Brian Tripp stated, "For me, it's like the alphabet."

The selection of pieces for this book and the exhibition from which it was drawn was based on three factors. First, we wanted to present Native Californian basketry as a regional body of work. We strove to include various types of baskets from all over California made from a broad range of materials and utilizing many different weaving techniques. Secondly, we hoped to present native basketry as documented works by known individuals rather than anonymous ethnic or tribal art. We have succeeded to the extent that a majority of the pieces are documented or attributable to specific weavers. Thirdly, we wanted to present native basketry as a living art form, part of a continuum of traditions and community histories hundreds and thousands of years in the making.

In this book we have tried to articulate something of the artistic and aesthetic qualities of Native Californian basketry. But we hope that the exposure and experience carries the reader beyond the objects, into a greater understanding of and appreciation for the indigenous cultures from which they sprang. A basket tells us so much more than "beauty" or "function": it reveals a history, a home, a tradition. It offers testimony to the intimate relationship between weaver and environment. This assemblage of values continues to inspire weavers and touch the rest of us with delight and wonder.

Brian Bibby
Guest Curator

TWO EARLY BASKETS

Maria Marta (Chumash) c. 1766–1830
PRESENTATION BASKET
c. 1822

split juncus stalks (field), split sumac shoots (white), split and dyed bulrush root (black), juncus stalks (foundation)
H. 6¼" Diam. 15⅞"
Phoebe A. Hearst Museum of Anthropology, University of California, Berkeley

This remarkable piece, nearly 175 years old, is one of the oldest examples of California Indian basketry for which the name of the weaver has survived. In fact, her name is woven into the rim of the basket. But anything else we know about her is largely due to the meticulous record-keeping of the Franciscans. She was apparently born in 1766, three years before the first European land expedition into California, at *s'omɘs*, a coastal village near present-day Ventura. In 1782 the Spaniards established Mission San Buenaventura there. Maria Marta's name appears in the mission's Book of Baptisms on June 5, 1788. Her native name was recorded as Laputimeu, her age at the time as twenty-one.

In 1821, when Maria Marta was in her mid-fifties, Mexico gained independence from Spain, and the next year Mexican General José de la Cruz arrived at Mission San Buenaventura where he was presented with this basket. The basket is remarkably fine, not only in the size of its foundation and its weft strands, which measure 320 weft strands per square inch, but in its reproduction of several images found on the Spanish peso in use at the time. Maria Marta reproduces the image of the Crown and Shield flanked by Pillars of Hercules an image that led these one-ounce silver coins to be nicknamed "pillar dollars" when they became legal tender in the early American Republic. There is also a Spanish inscription woven into the basket's rim: "Maria Marta Neofita De La Mision

De El Serafico Doctor San Buenaventura Me Hizo An." Translated, it reads, "Maria Marta, neophyte of the Mission of the Seraphic Doctor Buenaventura, made me yr." The word *año* (year) has not been completed; Maria Marta apparently ran out of room before she could weave in the date.

This basket was found in Mexico City in 1920 by Zelia Nuttall, who later donated it to the University of California's Museum of Anthropology (presently the Phoebe A. Hearst Museum of Anthropology). There are only five known Chumash baskets of this type extant in the United States.

Frank LaPena: "From an artist's point of view, the ability to replicate that kind of a design on a curved surface is pretty damn good—it really shows the technical ability of the weaver. If something has traditional form, you say, Oh, well, that's tradition, they do that automatically. But with this basket, you see something that is not of the weaver's own culture and it still shows her capabilities! The technical proficiency captures my imagination."

Frank Tuttle: "What intrigues me are the letters that serve as symbols, in the same fashion as the coin. The idea of borrowing symbols and re-inventing them, using them and bringing them into one's own personal space—that is the realm of the artist. From an artist's point of view, I'd say that is our job."

Frank LaPena: "You always have that question about contemporary Indian art: What are they doing, taking all these different kinds of images around them and using them in their art? With this basket we have an opportunity to look back in time and see that they were doing the same thing that contemporary artists do today. But with this perspective of time, we can recognize lots of things about it that are artistic, that are valid, and we call it traditional."

Craig Bates: "At the time this basket was made, this design style was at least thirty years old. It was part of the whole Chumash basket export business. The Vancouver voyage mentions this type of basket in 1792. Around the same time, when the Malaspina Expedition came to Monterey, the people there sent south to get Chumash baskets to give to the expedition. Many of the old Spanish families—people of means in Mexico and Peru who were connected with the *presidios* and other things in California—ended up with Chumash baskets. So quite early on, the Chumash were making, I don't know if you'd call it 'export art', but baskets that would appeal to foreigners. The industry of making baskets for non-Indians was already very well established by the time this basket was made."

Judith Polanich: "What I find interesting in this discussion is that, although the artists who have commented on this basket have talked about the challenge of adapting the flat coin motif to a curved surface, it's also adapted in a very Chumash way. The overall aspect of the basket is very Chumash. The coin design is in the body of the basket, just like a more traditional design would have been. And it's alternated around the basket just like a traditional design would have been. The band at the top and the filler designs all fit into a Chumash design layout that is completely traditional, even though the coin design itself isn't. The weaver is incorporating something new into a very Chumash sort of sensibility."

Artist Unknown (Pomo)
GIFT/STORAGE BASKET
c. 1840

split sedge root (buff), split and dyed bulrush root (black), willow shoots (foundation),
acorn woodpecker crest feathers, clamshell disc beads, glass beads
H. 13" Diam. 30"
Peabody Museum of Archaeology and Ethnology, Harvard University

Large coiled or twined baskets were sometimes made for gifts and exchanges between families at weddings, funerals, and other important occasions. Among the Pomo, the mother and sister of the bride would present such a basket to the mother or sister of the groom. Pomoan basketry displays many types of diagonal patterns, but there are some standard ideas that many weavers followed. One major characteristic is the offsetting of opposing triangles, which are intersected by a checkered (or other similar) pattern. When viewed from the top, looking down into the basket, the pattern appears as a dazzling swirling design.

This basket was collected by William Dane Phelps, master of the ship *Alert*, which sailed from Boston to California in 1840. Between 1840 and 1842 he made nine trips along the coast between San Francisco and San Diego, with stops at Monterey and Los Angeles, to acquire hides and tallow from the extensive California cattle herds, as well as the occasional otter hide from the dwindling population of fur-bearing mammals. In 1841 he made two trips up the Sacramento River to New Helvetia (Sutter's Fort) where he was entertained by John Augustus Sutter. Phelps later noted: "My good friends...had collected a great many beautiful articles of Indian manufacture, such as fine woven ornamental baskets . . .which they kindly forced me to accept . . . ." The Peabody Museum at Harvard University holds six baskets that were collected by Phelps in California in 1841. There are only about fifty pre–gold rush baskets from Northern and Central California presently known to exist in the United States.

Craig Bates: "For a coiled basket of this shape, it's really big! What also strikes me is that it's almost a hundred years before you find baskets of this shape and size made again."

Kathy Wallace: "When I look at something that big, as a basketweaver, I'm thinking of the hours of collecting, of processing, of sorting, of trimming your materials. And I look at this one and I think, That's what I want to do some day. But I realize how much energy and how much dedication it takes.

"I always have to turn Pomo baskets upside down to view the work put into them. When viewed from the side, the design looks totally different than when it's viewed from the top or bottom."

Judith Polanich: "Well, this is a basket that plays with your mind, too. This is one of those baskets where the dark and the light areas of the pattern are completely equal. So you've got two readings of it, depending on what you decide is the background. You can read it either as a light pattern on a dark background or a dark pattern on a light background. It's one of those baskets that shifts back and forth visually."

Frank LaPena "That richness, looking down into it, is really nice."

BURDEN BASKETS

Artist Unknown (Pomo)
BURDEN BASKET
c. 1890

split sedge root (buff), split winter redbud shoots (reddish), willow shoots (foundation)
H. 20¼" Diam. 21½"
State of California, Department of Parks and Recreation

Burden baskets were made and used throughout California. Grass seeds, acorns, greens, bulbs, and any variety of foods or other items were gathered and transported in baskets like these.

Most burden baskets were conical with wide mouths for easy filling. (The wide opening was especially useful in harvesting grass seeds with a seed beater.) Burden baskets were designed for heavy use: the basket rested in a large mesh net—generally encompassing the bottom two-thirds of the basket—which included a tumpline for carrying it. The tumpline fit across the top of the forehead, and the basket itself fit nicely against the back and shoulders. Maximum weight was distributed to the area of the upper back and shoulders, much as with a modern backpack.

This basket was collected by Charles P. Wilcomb at Kelseyville on the south side of Clear Lake in the first decade of the twentieth century.

Kathy Wallace: "I'm always taken by Pomo burden baskets. Their form is so unique, everything is always in such balance, and I'm amazed at the beauty that's put into a utility object. And this one is the epitome."

Craig Bates: "The shape is so beautiful, this elegant bell shape, and yet it doesn't seem to have been used by groups other than the Pomo—it's restricted to a really small area. And this idea of changing the weaving in the middle of a pattern is restricted, too, so far as I know, to the Pomo and then the Costanoan people below San Francisco. These weavers change technique while making the serrations on the upper diamonds. They change from diagonal twining to plain twining in order to produce a straight vertical line, to get those serrations good and straight."

Judith Polanich: "It's quite unusual for a weaver to switch technique in the middle of a course of weaving. But to make this pattern right, you have to do it. The diagonal line is made by the diagonal twining itself; it will do it for you without any problem. But it won't do the straight, vertical edge, so you have to switch to plain twining. "

Denise Davis: "That's something I think about all the time. I have tried to push my lines, my edges, to make them really sharp. You know, I want this edge really sharp, so I'll do double stitches sometimes. When you're taught weaving, these artistic things aren't explained. I believe they come with time."

Frank LaPena: "I think as an artist or a weaver who's doing his or her own work, you already have a sense of what you want to do. You think, How am I going to do this? And then you just do it. Later on others might wonder, Why did she do that?"

Judith Polanich: "That little serration, I don't see it below the upper wall. It's just on those top two designs. It's really interesting. As an artist, what does she want that serration to do? What does that serration accomplish, visually?"

Frank Tuttle: "Why would an artist do that? I would do it because at that point, at the wide space in this beautiful bell shape, the black and white needs visual relief. One design unit begins to assert itself over another. At a certain point the clear distinction between a light pattern and a dark pattern [weakens]: something needs to occur. Oftentimes it's just like a line in drawing or painting. A line is so immediate and so informative: it can be straight and delineated and sharp and climb or slope, or it can be soft and smudged and transitory. And that's what's occurring here, to my eye, from a painter's point of view.

"Another thing intrigues me about these shapes. To be able to see these baskets out on the hillside with that [tumpline] net [around them]. I mean, that would be a completely unique thing to see on a hillside near a bush. All these wonderful [natural] shapes that we take for granted so often—and then all of the sudden here's this magnificent zigzagging shape! I always think back to the description of the building of Bidwell's chimney, where the women brought the bricks in burden baskets. Talk about impact! An impact that is visual as well as technical!"

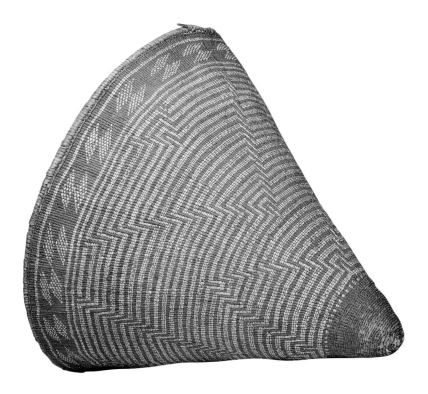

Artist Unknown (Wailaki)

BURDEN BASKET
c. 1890

split conifer root (buff), bear grass (white), willow shoots (foundation)
H. 19½" Diam. 19"
State of California, Department of Parks and Recreation

The Wailaki people lived in villages located throughout much of the Eel River drainage and surrounding country in what is now Mendocino County. In traditional times the Wailaki consisted of nineteen linguistically related yet distinct groups. Little is known about Wailaki weaving traditions, and few documented examples of their basketry exist in either museum or private collections.

Traditional Wailaki basketry that has survived is primarily twined: weft elements, usually split conifer roots, are plain-twined around warp rods of willow, hazel, or some other shoot material. Bear grass is used in a full twist overlay technique to produce design elements.

The use of an overlay of light-toned bear grass on a dark conifer-root background to ornament everyday work baskets is widely distributed throughout California. This Wailaki example uses nearly equal portions of light and dark to create a binary visual effect, so that either the light or the dark may be read as the design. Burden baskets from this region traditionally make use of a separate border design.

Denise Davis: "When you get farther away from this basket. . .the diagonal motif just bounces out at you. Which I love with paintings! When I see paintings that are big and they hit me like that, from across the room, it's effective artistically. If I was standing outside the door, I would see that diagonal standing out, the optical illusion. It is really beautiful from that perspective."

Frank LaPena: "I think another thing that's important about this basket is the way its energy works. Compare it to the energy in the [Pomo] basket we just looked at. With that piece, the dark and light and also the form are complex, so you get that real fast. With this one, you get an appreciation for it in another way, a more subtle way. And yet, at the same time, it works because it is dark and light and because it has horizontal repetition. When that changes, that's where you get this whole play of energy coming through. I like that. What happens is you are dealing with rectangular forms, and the repetition of those forms gives you the complexity. This is the kind of complexity you see in Bridget Riley's work. It's that same kind of thing. It's the idea of the repetition giving you the complexity. But the subtle coloring elevates it, in my mind, to the same level as the Pomo piece. And the complexity is not only the shape, because when you start changing the form . . . that drags you into it even more. That's what modern art does. That's what Bridget Riley does. That's what this piece does."

Judith Polanich: "The other thing that the line shift accomplishes . . . just look at the part where the design is only horizontal and try to imagine the whole basket like that. Without that shift, if you only have the horizontal pattern, the basket almost collapses. With that shift, it gives a real solidity to the basket and a real sense of volume. It rounds out the wall so you have a sense of the basket as a container."

Lori Smith: "This is one of those baskets where the design changes right before your eyes and something else will jump out at you. It must have been hard to keep track of this design. There's a series of designs going on. You really can't see this diagonal pattern unless you get back from it. It almost looks like that three-dimensional, vibrating stuff.

"In regards to the shape, I think it's obvious that the weaver had to get lots of sticks in the bottom right away to flare it out. This basket, I'll bet, probably has a thousand sticks in it. And a lot of these the basketmaker has to get in right away because it flares out so suddenly. It's so even. It's almost a perfect cone. Also, if you add all those sticks right away, it makes a very solid, heavy bottom with all the triple weave and all the sticks; it's real stout."

Vivien Hailstone: "No basket is made without thought. You have to know what design you're going to make right from the beginning."

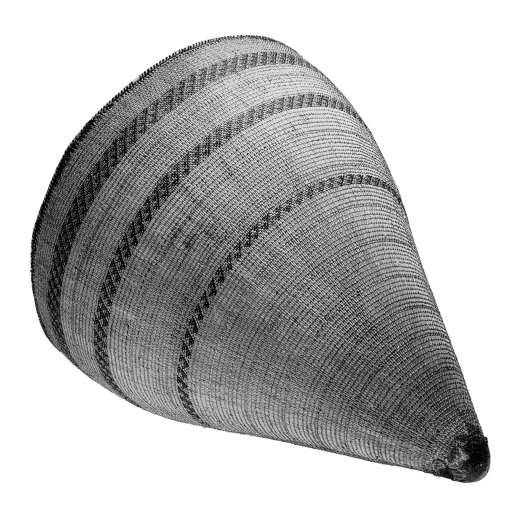

Artist Unknown (Western Mono)
BURDEN BASKET
c. 1910

sourberry shoots (foundation), split winter redbud (reddish), split sedge root (buff)
H. 26 ⅛" Diam. 21 ¾"
The Field Museum of Natural History

The Western Mono (or Monache) are six distinct groups of people related by language and culture and living in the Sierra foothill region of Madera and Fresno Counties. They are closely related to the Paiute people from east of the Sierra, and their weaving and basketry traditions are similarly related. In addition to twined baskets for gathering and processing a substantial variety of native foods, the Western Mono also produce coiled basketry. In the past thirty years, they have probably been one of the most active groups making traditional baskets in California.

Judith Polanich: "There aren't many of these. Burden baskets—used primarily for acorn gathering—were one of the first forms to disappear among the Western Mono. They were so labor-intensive and so easily replaced by gunny sacks and other containers. The sticks that you had to gather for this! A weaver once told me that it took two or three years of gathering to have enough sticks—all very fine and perfectly matched in size—to make a basket like this. There weren't many made later on because of that.

"All Western Mono twined ware has banded patterns. The designs themselves are counted so they're all even. In Western Mono twining, all the warp additions are put in by counting. You can go around the basket and see that a stick is added, say, every third stick or every fifth. The Pomo put them in whenever they think they need to, for shape, not by count. [Regularity] is important for the Western Mono, because so many of their baskets are parallel warp, and the two sides of the basket have to be kept even. That's another reason that the sticks have to be perfect. It's a very different way of doing things [from the Pomo], and it works for the Western Mono because the design units themselves are so very small. You don't have to worry about covering a large space. You've got a very small finite design. And again, within the design, you have equal patches of dark and light."

Craig Bates: "The neat thing about this is that the materials allow you to do something you can't do with other materials. Because the sedge is so strong and the sourberry sticks compress so much, you can get away without doing close twining, like the Western Mono's neighbors on the east side of the Sierra did. The use of different materials, ones that are available only to west-side people, allows them to do something similar [to close twining], yet really unique and different."

Western Mono woman with burden basket and tumpline, c. 1910. Courtesy State of California Department of Parks and Recreation.

Artist Unknown (Achumawi)
BURDEN BASKET
c. 1895

split conifer root (interior weft), bear grass (white), split winter redbud shoots (reddish), willow shoots (foundation)
H. 19½" Diam. 22½"
The Redding Museum of Art and History

The term Achumawi has been used historically to include nine "bands" of linguistically related peoples living along the Pit River drainage in northeastern California. The term is used here because of the lack of documentation about the provenance of this particular piece. Basketry from the Pit River area is exclusively twined, using split pine root as the primary weft element, and bear grass and/or maidenhair fern as overlay materials. Burden baskets from the Pit River region were apparently quite popular with non-Indian collectors and buyers, and there are large collections of Achumawi baskets throughout the country. Some weavers made scaled-down burden basket models that were sold as cornucopias for table arrangements in American homes.

Frank Tuttle: "In the various large conical burden baskets, from a painter's point of view, what speaks to me is how the motif is utilized and how the motif will speak to a viewer in terms of its 'speed' [visual perception of movement]. If you recall the Pomo burden basket, it swirls on a spiral; it's such a strong movement over that conical form, enveloping that container. The Wailaki [basket] had that very subtle, wonderful, almost computerized fret-step pattern that was very slow. It did a very tricky play with the eye, where the motif is very subtle, very uniform—it's deceptive in that way. The Mono basket had that airiness of a volume that transitions from inside to outside, that sense of being able to look through a transparency there. And then this one, with its step pattern, the bold black and white, again reinforcing a conical shape. It moves at a different pace from the others. It moves in a different direction. It's like painters—me, Brian [Tripp], Frank [LaPena]—using the same materials: it's how we manipulate that material, manipulate similar motifs, and are able to say what we want to say personally. A reflection of where we're coming from, of regional similarities and differences."

Brian Tripp: "I love that black outline. It just makes it more elegant. It just makes that dark set up."

Frank Tuttle: "And the little gestural things, I enjoy those, those little personal statements. On an object that every household may have had at one point."

Kathy Wallace: "Doesn't it flare out where the line goes across? When you're weaving and you're adding sticks, it's much easier to add in a horizontal line of color. You have to be careful not to interfere with the design. So the design limits where you can add."

SEED BEATERS, HOPPERS, AND WINNOWERS

Mary (Southern Miwuk) c. 1840–c. 1923
SEED BEATER
c. 1905

creek dogwood shoots (reddish), split buck brush shoots (buff), deer brush shoots (buff)
H. 7⅜" Diam. 9⅝" Length 13⅜"
The Yosemite Museum, National Park Service

When the woman who came to be known as "Indian Mary" was born, it was still some ten years before any non-Indian would enter Yosemite Valley. By the time she died, Yosemite Valley was a place that included automobiles, hotels, electricity, and telephones.

Daughter of Captain Paul, whose position of leadership she seems to have inherited, Mary was about eleven years old when the Mariposa Battalion entered Yosemite Valley in March of 1851. It is not certain whether she was part of the group living in the valley at that time, but Mary and her family were known to spend the winter months in the Bull Creek area. At the turn of the century she lived in a small cabin near the base of Sentinel Rock.

Mary, who spent much of her adult life in Yosemite Valley, maintaining close friendships with many of Yosemite's new residents, was adept at making nearly every type of Miwuk twined and coiled basket. In her later years Mary made several baskets that were destined for the tourist market in Yosemite. She derived her livelihood from posing for photographs and selling her baskets.

This basket is an adaptation of an older style seed beater and was probably made to be sold. Seed beaters were traditionally used as flails to knock a variety of seeds loose from various grass stalks and small shrubs into the open mouth of a burden basket. The typical Sierra Miwuk seed beaters were made in an open-work twined fashion. In this piece the design has been formed by leaving the reddish bark on the creek dogwood shoots and bunching them next to the cleanly scraped deer brush shoots.

Frank LaPena: "I like the idea that the material itself is the design. A very direct, very honest kind of work. The form is obviously related to its function, and by using the colors and just letting it be what it is, it's very integrated, it's very honest, it's very direct."

L. Frank Manriquez: "It's real easy in art to overwork things. You want to manipulate the medium, you want to have control, control, control. Here, the function dictates the design. It is nice when things are taken out of your hands."

Vivien Hailstone: "This is a basket that you wear out quickly because you're using it a lot, so you don't put in all the fancy designs. This is a basket that's easily woven."

Craig Bates: "There was a tremendous demand on those Yosemite women to make baskets because there were so many visitors wanting to buy them. Baskets like this could be made up really fast, in about six hours. Using these unpeeled shoots, which make a nice effect, and usually are creek dogwood shoots, makes the basket go so much quicker too, because you don't have to scrape your sticks."

Judith Polanich: "This form makes sense as a response to market. For one thing, you're not going to get an awful lot of seed-gathering after the turn of the century. There was no trespassing on farms and ranches. People weren't allowed free access to seed lands."

Frank Tuttle: "For me as a painter, someone whose pieces aren't always two-dimensional, and often protrude into the viewer's space, what I enjoy about these pieces is the whole notion that they are containers, that there is a volume that's being contained.

Mary, c. 1885. Courtesy of California State Library.

As an artist, when I'm manipulating materials, I recognize these materials as familiar to my tribal background; and yet at other times these materials may be no more than colored polymers. This half-melon shape with the little handle is wonderful—as a shape and as a further solution to the container problem."

Denise Davis: "Also, it's a sculpture. There's a lot of texture there. There's a form, plus there's this wonderful weave that's moving through the piece."

Minnie Reed (Yurok) 1889–1985

HOPPER MORTAR BASKET

c. 1955

split conifer root (buff), bear grass (white), hazel shoots (foundation)
H. 6⅞" Diam. 17"
Collection of Vivien Hailstone

The Yurok have lived for centuries in permanent villages along the lower Klamath River. Their houses, which usually had names, were constructed of redwood planks, and were rectangular, semi-subterranean structures containing two or more levels. Redwood was also used for transportation: a single redwood trunk was carved out to create a substantial dugout canoe used in traveling to neighboring villages along the river. The Yurok have been among the most prolific California basketmakers of the nineteenth and twentieth centuries.

Minnie Harry Reed, who created this basket, was born and raised in the ancient Yurok town of Morek, along the lower Klamath River. She began making baskets when she was about eight years old. Her daughter, Christina Ipiña, remembers her as a woman of strong will, who raised four children after the death of her husband in 1937, providing for her family by catching fish in the Klamath River, raising vegetables in her garden, and selling her basketry. The money she earned from the sale of baskets eventually helped put a daughter through nursing school.

The hopper mortar basket was used in acorn preparation. It was set over a stone mortar hole to help keep particles of acorn meat from escaping while pounding was taking place. It also helped keep foreign particles from blowing into the pounding

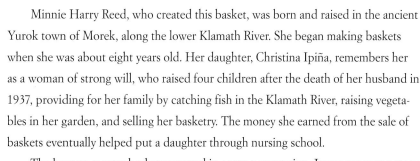

Minnie Reed, c. 1910. Courtesy of Christine Reed Ipiña.

-27-

area and mixing with the acorn. The horizontal rods, attached by a lattice weave, offered strength and bracing against the weight of the woman's calves, which rested on either side of the basket's rim while pounding was in progress.

Vivien Hailstone: "This basket's wrapped toward the bottom and on the top, because it gets really hard use. It's made with big materials. Usually for the utility baskets in our area, we don't use the black [maidenhair fern stem], because it wears off easy. We just use the bear grass overlay, which is really tough."

Brian Tripp: "One of the things I was told is, when you're using this kind of basket, you don't look down in the hole 'cause it will shorten your life. See, if you're using it, you'd have something in it [acorns]. But you don't take it and look through it. Madeline [Davis] told me that."

Kathy Wallace: "This hopper is made of sturdy materials for rough use, but it still has a lovely pattern in the subtle tones of a utility basket."

Artist Unknown (Chumash)
WINNOWING/GENERAL UTILITY TRAY
c. 1800–1850

split juncus stalks (field), split and dyed juncus (black), split sumac shoots (white), juncus stalks (foundation)
H. 5" Diam. 18½"
Peabody Museum of Archaeology and Ethnology, Harvard University

The Chumash formerly used winnowing trays like this for separating the chaff from a variety of seeds. The seedheads were rubbed against the basket and then tossed in the air; the wind carried away the chaff, while the heavier seeds fell back into the deep tray. Collection records indicate this basket was obtained at or near Santa Ynez.

Kathy Wallace: "I'm not a juncus user, but they're some of my favorite baskets because the variation in color adds a whole new texture to the design. It has a shadowed kind of texture, rather than being one even color. I really like that."

Judith Polanich: "This is certainly representative of an earlier style, pre-1900, rather than the later simplified Chumash style."

Craig Bates: "Some Western art historians claim you can look at native women artists the same way you look at Western artists like Monet or painters like that. An argument I have [with that view] is that a lot of the women who do really innovative work sometimes return to their earlier styles, thirty, forty, fifty years later. You can't really tell, say, a Carrie Bethel basket of 1929 from a Carrie Bethel basket of 1959, or even 1970, because the same kinds of things will often be repeated. I think this may be a good example of how women who learned and started making this style of basket in their youth, perhaps in the late eighteenth century, just kept making the same style until they died sometime in the nineteenth century."

Brian Tripp: "Well that's the thing that's put on us artists now. You're supposed to be innovative and keep changing all the time; but hey, you find something that works for you, that's good, and you keep doing it. I have favorite designs that I use all the time."

Sarah Knight (Pomo) c. 1845–1913
WINNOWING/SIFTING TRAY
1906

split sedge root (buff), split winter redbud shoots (reddish), willow shoots (foundation)
H. 3⅞" Diam. 15⅜"
The Field Museum of Natural History

Sarah Knight was probably from the village of *lema*, which was located south of Ukiah. She was married twice: first to John Knight, one of the earliest non-Indian settlers in the Ukiah area and owner of one of the largest ranches in the region; then to Pete Lamarr, a Pomo man from Lake County, who was later murdered.

Sarah Knight specialized in plain and lattice twining techniques, as evidenced by the winnowing tray and open-work lattice-twined storage basket visible in the photograph. Her work is characterized by unusually fine, evenly sized warp and weft elements.

Bands of lattice twining, a technique that incorporates a laterally running rod over the vertical warp rods, are also found in four separate bands on the winnower. These bands are generally woven into winnowing and sifting trays for added strength.

Among the Pomo, this style of basket usually has a design layout scheme of three or four horizontal bands. Each design band generally makes use of different motifs, although occasionally all design bands will be the same. In this example, as in many others, the design bands make equal use of light and dark.

Sarah Knight's daughter, Mary Knight Benson, became one of the finest and most famous Pomo weavers, mastering several twining and coiling techniques. Sarah Knight and Mary Benson maintained a steady business relationship with American Indian art dealer Grace Nicholson, for whom many of their baskets were made.

Sherrie Smith-Ferri: "It's a very old-fashioned basket, a real classic design with that banded pattern and the alternating dark and light design elements. Very nice work, very even, very elegant. It's deceptively simple."

Frank Tuttle: "For me, an important part of the sifters, especially Pomo sifters like this one, is the shape. I can imagine the actual object itself. It doesn't have a flat bottom. So the design we see here [from this side] is more of an ovoid shape, unless we look directly down on it; then we get the strong concentric circles. I always enjoy that, the way the circular pattern just all of a sudden squishes out, it's flat. It's a heavy duty bit of work with that lattice in there. I don't know if this one was made for use or not, but I know that other sifters when they're made for use with acorn stuff, they get a real workout. They just start flappin' around. The design elements are two rows in that first band of designs, alternating dark and light. A large zone of no color, then that next one where the pattern sets. It sets sort of on a vertical. Then that last row of color has three rows, and it's much larger. The band increases in size and adds to that circular, radiating effect."

Sherrie Smith-Ferri: "I think it's important to note that Sarah Knight was the mother of Mary Benson, who was probably the most famous Pomo basketweaver. One of the hallmarks of Mary Benson's work is its fineness and evenness and its great regularity, and you see the same attention to quality and the same characteristics of fineness and evenness in this Sarah Knight basket."

Sarah Knight. Courtesy of The Field Museum of Natural History.

Lucy Baker (Maidu) 1859–1920

WINNOWING TRAY
1907

split maple shoots (white), split winter redbud shoots (reddish), dyed bracken root (black), willow shoots (foundation)
H. 3" Diam. 16½"
Department of Anthropology, Smithsonian Institution

The Maidu, who have made their homes in the high meadows and valleys of the Sierra Nevada for centuries, are renowned for their weaving. Lucy Baker, who lived in Indian Valley, north of Quincy, produced baskets that can be found in the Smithsonian Institution and the Field Museum (Chicago). Lucy Baker's granddaughter, Lilly Baker, now in her eighties, is also a weaver. She remembers as a youngster watching her grandmother "fixing material" for her baskets. Lilly has served as a teacher and mentor for contemporary Maidu weaver Denise Davis (see page 35).

A winnowing basket such as the one pictured was probably used for more than just winnowing: it might also have been used for holding acorn meats during the shelling and cleaning process. The central design layout, based on three points, was a popular scheme used throughout northeastern California. Maiduan coiled basketry is universally made on a three-rod foundation, often using split willow or maple shoots as weft elements for the neutral background tone. Split winter redbud shoots and bracken roots were used for the dark contrasting weft elements.

Craig Bates: "One thing that strikes me about this basket is that it's basically an old-style pattern that's been changed by using two colors in the design. It's part of the new genre of baskets that's really rampant among the people in the mountains by 1915, when they're making so much of this stuff for sale to non-Indians. That changed the old conventions of using just one color in the pattern. It's kind of neat in that she's changed it subtly without changing the pattern."

Frank LaPena: "If you start looking at these points and this shape, the movement in this basket seems to be going almost every which way. The kind of energy that's running around is really nice. It has a really good sense of holding your attention."

Denise Davis: "Whenever you make a painting of baskets with these kind of designs, you want to contort the triangles to get the same feeling as when you weave them. Because, you know, in baskets, the way they're designed, they're not flat triangles. But the technology of how you make them gives you that illusion. They're kind of fluid, they're like water or something."

Brian Tripp: "That's a good word to use, 'fluid'."

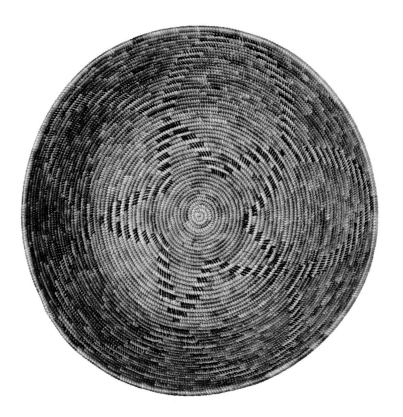

Artist Unknown (Kumeyaay)

TRAY
1914

split juncus stalks (field), juncus stalks (foundation), split sumac shoots (white), split devil's claw (black)
H. 3 ⅞" Diam. 13 ¾"
The Field Museum of Natural History

The Kumeyaay, formerly known as Diegueño and later as Ipai-Tipai, maintain communities on both sides of the U.S.-Mexico border. Many still speak Kumeyaay as a first language and Spanish as a second. The traditional Kumeyaay homeland includes both interior desert and coastal environments. People migrated throughout the year, moving from the valley floor or canyon bottom to work their way gradually into the higher elevations of the mountains, following the ripening of various plant foods. Six varieties of acorns, as well as a variety of other plants, could be collected within the Kumeyaay habitat. The Kumeyaay used pottery for cooking and storage, as well as baskets for collecting and processing foods.

This basket was collected at Mesa Grande in 1914. The alternating of light and dark materials within the design scheme was a popular strategy in several parts of southern California.

Frank LaPena: "The idea of getting that design by alternating the material is really nice."

Brian Bibby: "Do you think that's a way to maximize the contrast?"

Frank LaPena: "Yes, to bring up that sense of an integrated whole as it flows through the entire design from top to bottom."

L. Frank Manriquez: "When I look at this basket, the most elaborate stories begin weaving in my mind. The design gently but firmly pulls you into the 'artistic idea' place."

Bertha Mitchell (Wintun) 1934–
WINNOWING TRAY
1970

split spring redbud shoots (white), split winter redbud shoots (reddish), willow shoots (foundation)
H. 3⅛" Diam. 17⅝"
Collection of Mr. & Mrs. Chris Ehrke

Bertha Wright Mitchell was born in the old village of *tlet* in Colusa County. A significant portion of her childhood and adolescence was spent around her grandparents who spoke only the old Wintun language. Bertha's grandmother, Lyda Buck, and mother, Mollie Wright, were basketmakers. By the age of nine Bertha was making her own baskets. Her method of learning was through observation. Bertha stated that she wasn't taught to weave but learned how by watching her mother. Bertha recalled, "I thought it was boring." But eventually she "just felt like doing it. I just had it in me to do it."

As is often the case in a conservative community or family where traditional ties are strong, Bertha's basketry is much like her mother and grandmother's work. Some baskets are very nearly identical. "I never copied anybody else's design; it was all my mother's. My grandmother did the same design over and over." In this winnowing tray, Bertha has chosen a design motif she calls "quail tops." She refers to his type of tray as *k'enni'*.

Bertha lives in Arbuckle and has recently taken on an apprentice to teach traditional Wintun basketry. She is also one of the very few remaining fluent speakers of the Cortina Wintun language.

Frank LaPena: "I like the boldness. It fits what it could be used for."

L. Frank Manriquez: "There's almost a sense of urgency with this basket."

Craig Bates: "One thing that I think is remarkable is that here's this basket being made by a woman who is about thirty-six years old, and the basket is identical to things being made two generations earlier."

Brian Bibby: "Note how the design steadily grows in dimension as the basket progresses in diameter. It creates the illusion of spinning the basket."

Bertha Mitchell, 1995. Photograph by Brian Bibby.

Artist Unknown (Washoe)

SIFTING TRAY
c. 1910

split willow shoots (buff), dyed bracken root (black), willow shoots (foundation)
H. 4" Diam. 16" Length 19"
The Haggin Museum

The ovoid shape of this basket is typical of Washoe close-twined sifting trays. The small end is held toward the body when used for sifting acorn flour. The finely pounded flour sticks to the twined weave while the coarser granules roll off. The basket is then turned upside down and tapped, with the finished flour falling into another basket.

In former times the Washoe made their homes on the eastern slope of the Sierra Nevada and into the Great Basin, an area of harsh, bitterly cold winters and hot dry summers. Grass seeds, piñon pine nuts, fish, and various mammals were part of the traditional diet. Groups of Washoe often traveled over to the west slope of the Sierra to gather acorns and other desired goods. They used the Lake Tahoe area as their traditional summer camp for trading and taking advantage of various alpine resources. Today there are four Washoe colonies: one in California, at Woodfords (Alpine County); and three in Nevada, at Dresslerville, Carson, and Reno.

Frank LaPena: "The design on here is really neat, where the weaver shifts the positive and negative."

Craig Bates: "Because [in weaving] you flip the basket over every time you reach the right margin so that you always have the half-rounded side of the split willow facing you while you weave, that means on the basket you get alternating rows of the sap-wood and split-face sides of the sewing strand. One side will be the sap-wood; the other will be the split side. The split side is rougher and more porous, and tends to attract dirt. Thus, the shiny, smoother surface and the rougher, duller surface contrast, and that gives you those subtle lines. That middle band is "sunburned" willow, which is really kind of a second-choice design material. It's the inner bark of the willow adhering to the split willow shoots. It abrades easily and thus wasn't always preferred for patterns."

Denise Davis (Maidu) 1956–
SIFTING TRAY
1992

split big leaf maple shoots (white), split winter redbud shoots (reddish), willow shoots (foundation)
H. 1¼" Diam. 12½"
Collection of Carl Mautz

Denise's ancestors made their home in the large mountain meadows of Plumas County near the settlement of Genessee. In 1986 she began learning under the tutelage of elder Maidu weaver Lilly Baker. An active weaver, Denise has become familiar with the many nuances of gathering the natural materials that have been used by generations of Maidu weavers. She also received

instruction from Pomo/Patwin master weaver Mabel McKay. Recently Denise has taught weaving to several women of various tribal backgrounds in northern California, helping to reintroduce traditional basketmaking in their communities. She is also a fine contemporary artist and printmaker.

Denise Davis: "I paint, too, so I'm always playing with the designs. With this basket I was playing with the white, trying to think to myself while I was weaving it that the white was actually the design. I was playing with the white, using it as I would the red. And that's why it bounces from the middle all the way out, from darkness to light, and dances off the edge, off the white rim on the outside. Lilly [Baker] said we always have to have a white rim around the edge."

Denise Davis, 1992. Photograph by Hank Meals.

Amanda Wilson (Konkow) c. 1864–1946
SIFTING TRAY
c. 1940

split sedge root (buff), split and dyed briar root (black), willow shoots (foundation)
Diam. 15⅞"
Collection of Craig D. Bates

Amanda Wilson was an influential woman in her community. Her father was Pomaho, a headman who had signed the 1851 treaty with the United States. Amanda also married a headman, Holai Lafonso. She had two children with him and, later, a daughter, Eva, from a second marriage, to Santa Wilson. At the village of Mikchopdo, Amanda was a leader in the women's dance society, a highly respected organization with membership only by invitation and initiation. She was a close friend of Annie Bidwell, and after the collapse of the sacred dance society she was an active and dedicated worker in the Presbyterian Church. One of the only two known examples of nontraditional baskets woven by Amanda was a chalice-shaped piece made for a local Presbyterian minister (the other was a coiled basket reminiscent of a Datsolalee *degikup* or fancy basket). Baskets created by Amanda Wilson were collected by family members, native people from neighboring communities, and non-Indians (Bates & Bibby, 1984: 38-43).

This flat acorn flour sifting tray is in a typical Konkow style. To use it, a handful of meal is placed on the tray and the basket is tapped with the fingers. This separates the coarse granules from the fine flour, with the granules rolling off the edge of the sifter into an awaiting basket. The fine flour clinging to the corrugations of the coiled basket is then transferred to another basket by tapping the topside of the sifter with the fingers or a special "flour knocker" made of a small burl or knobbed stick.

This sifting basket and the receiving basket that follows were made as a set. The design motif in both baskets was a favorite of Amanda's. The motif is associated with valley quail topknots, which might explain its special appeal to Amanda, whose Konkow name, *oymutni*, means "sound made by a quail."

Harry Fonseca: "First of all, there's the shape: the roundness and flatness of it. And the idea of a spiral [foundation]: you don't read it right away; it almost looks like concentric circles, but it's actually a spiral, which is pretty dynamic. One interesting thing about this tray is that the design is divided up into quarters, four areas. There are little design elements right at the edge of the tray, and they just anchor the whole thing. The four little spots balance the entire inside.

"There are the four quail plume motifs in the center, then the clear area in the middle of the basket, then the four quail plume designs that take you out farther, then four more going in the opposite direction—really giving this design a lot of energy—and, of course, the last four that really, really grow. And then those little design elements—which actually look like the tops of quail plumes—that are part of the next set of designs, finishing off the whole thing. It's balanced so nicely, with the negative and positive space—really incredible when you look at it."

Brian Bibby: "One thing I hope readers of this book will see is the careful planning of the design layouts and the execution of the motifs themselves, the way they fill a particular shape and space. How do you, as an artist, deal with that space?"

Harry Fonseca: "As a painter, you do the same thing—when you're drawing a small sketch or you're working on a small piece of paper, say the size of a postcard, you take that size into consideration and the design that goes in it. And when you work on a large canvas, five by six feet, it's a whole different thing. In this basket, she's working with all of it. The center is smaller, and as the basket starts to get bigger, she starts to enlarge the design elements. Which happens in so many of the baskets—I look at them and I think, my god, how in the hell is this done? And that's just in terms of design. When you look at the actual technique and the energy the basket causes . . . . it's amazing! But it seems all the really good basketweavers have this design consciousness."

Amanda Wilson with granddaughter, Francis (Wilson) Potter, 1940. Courtesy of The Southwest Museum.

Amanda Wilson (Konkow) c. 1864–1946

ACORN FLOUR RECEIVING BASKET

c. 1940

split sedge root (buff), split and dyed briar root (black), willow shoots (foundation)
H. 5½" Diam. 9⅝"
Collection of Craig D. Bates

This basket, like the previous one, is made with briar root, a fairly uncommon material in basketmaking. Baskets made with briar root have a limited distribution, appearing mainly in the area around Chico. Briar root is naturally dark brown, but was often soaked in a solution made with valley oak galls or black walnut husks in order to darken the fiber to black.

Craig Bates: "To my knowledge, this is one of the only extant matched sets of baskets collected among the Konkow at Chico. It is a very fine example of Amanda Wilson's weaving style and was made for her daughter, Eva. The arrangement of the quail plume motif on this basket is very similar to two other trays she wove. I think it is one of those cases where a weaver works out a certain arrangement of a pattern, likes it, and keeps working with it over a period of time. It would be like a contemporary artist doing four or five paintings of the same image and labeling them numbers one, two, three, and so on.

"This pair of baskets is woven in Amanda Wilson's precise 'presentation' style, a much finer coiling than she used in weaving utilitarian baskets. It's obvious she tried to make these baskets especially fine examples of her weaving."

Artist Unknown (Yuki)
WINNOWING/GENERAL UTILITY BASKET
c. 1895

split spring redbud shoots (white), split winter redbud shoots (reddish), willow shoots? (foundation)
H. 7½" Diam. 23"
The Haggin Museum

Before the advent of Europeans in California, there were probably three separate groups of Yuki living in three different areas: along Mendocino coast, and in inland valleys along the middle and south forks of the Eel River. Their language has no known relatives. In 1856 one of the first federal reservations in the state was carved out of the heart of the Yuki homeland, in Round Valley. Over the next decade hundreds of native peoples from various parts of northern California were moved to Round Valley. This relocation of large numbers of people into their territory and the atrocious aggressions on Yuki people and lands by Euro-Americans had devastating effects on the indigenous population.

As a result, many aspects of Yuki basketry are poorly understood. Yuki coiled baskets have one unique feature: in most northern California basketry, the coil moves in a leftward direction, as the basket faces the weaver; Yuki coiling, on the other hand, moves in a rightward direction. The Yuki also practiced plain twining using split pine root weft elements for the making of hoppers, burden baskets, and acorn sifting baskets.

Large deep trays like this probably had more than one purpose. In addition to winnowing, this type of basket could be used for gathering or temporarily storing food and other items. When looking at the complex connecting pattern of this basket—which begins as a five-pointed star on the base and evolves into a network of parallel intersecting lines—it should be noted that weavers did not use predrawn graphs or any kind of permanent design layout form.

Craig Bates: "The pattern is a common one in central California, used by Miwuk, Maidu, Pomo, Patwin, Yuki, and probably other people. When compared to documented specimens made by the Yuki in other collections, this basket is exceptionally large and well woven. Too, it resembles some baskets collected from that small group of people living at the Northeastern Pomo village at Stonyford."

Frank Tuttle: "The way the design grows and spreads itself over the surface proportionally, it's a simple but effective use of materials and motif. How beautiful it must have been to have seen hints of the block pattern emerge from underneath the acorn meal—almost like mountains emerging from behind swirling, dissipating valley fog. This basket is another example of the fact that Yuki people existed—and still exist. To see this basket is real satisfying to me."

STORAGE BASKETS

Artist Unknown (Yurok / Karuk / Hupa)
STORAGE BASKET
c. 1895

split conifer root (buff), bear grass (white), hazel shoots? (foundation)
H. 24" Diam. 18½"
Department of Anthropology, Smithsonian Institution

Because of the weaving techniques and materials used, this basket is clearly recognizable as having been made in the vicinity of the Klamath-Trinity River region. Design schemes for Klamath River storage baskets were generally arranged in vertical patterns. The central motif appearing in this piece is a variation of what weavers from the region term "running" design or mark. Still, it is not possible to distinguish exact tribal origin without some kind of documentation.

Large twined baskets like this were formerly used to store a variety of items including acorns, grass seeds, and clothing. A burden basket sometimes served as a lid. Such baskets usually sat along the interior wall on one of the two or three levels of the semisubterranean redwood plank house. Ethnographer Lila M. O'Neale, who spent the summer of 1929 interviewing Yurok and Karuk weavers along the Klamath River and whose work resulted in the landmark publication *Yurok-Karok Basketweavers*, noted: "Indian women recalling memories of older days describe the better class house with its earth ledge at shoulder height. On it were set all sizes of covered baskets storing food supplies, clothing, and other belongings. Ideally, the sides of the room were lined with fine baskets, all full." (O'Neale, 1932:38)

The largeness of these storage baskets, O'Neale reports, forced the weaver to use somewhat different methods during the weaving process than were used for other baskets. And the baskets' size also apparently made quite an impression on youngsters. "A basket might be so large that the maker would have to stand to work on it. Informants sometimes tried to express their memories of fright when as children they had leaned over too far to find themselves heels over head in the big *chipnuks*." (O'Neale, 1932:39)

Brian Tripp: "The design of this one really hits my sensibility. I've always known it was called a friendship design. But I've heard it described as running marks, too.

"I like the way this basket is so wild-looking; it's got a real wild feel to it. It's like something I'd like to paint. Kind of loose, but at the same time very solid. Almost all the baskets from up in our area strive for perfection. They're so beautiful and so big and bold and nice and everything's just perfect. And then here's this one, just. . .ohhh. This is like what I strive for when I'm working, this kind of controlled chaos. When you put it back into our culture, that's basically what we're trying to do, control chaos. Here's a truly unique basket. Do you know how hard it is to do something totally wild and still make it feel right?"

Judith Polanich: "It's hard not to be delighted by the painterly, playful quality of the design in this piece."

L. Frank Manriquez: "To me, this one represents 'artist'. We're within our society, within our boundaries and our constraints, but inside there's this nuttiness. So while fitting into the tribe, the artist is allowed to express herself fully through her work."

Jean LaMarr: "That's what they say about a lot of artists who are craftsmen. They work so fine, they want to get away from that and do something very different."

Kathy Wallace: "One of the things to note is how sturdy this basket is on the bottom—they used big materials. The basket's going to be heavy when it's filled up with things to store. It's going to get wear and tear as you move it around, so it's very sturdy on the bottom. Then, when the design starts, after it's turned up, that's when the material gets smaller and finer."

Jennie Miller (Pomo) 1842–1932

STORAGE BASKET
c. 1900

split sedge root (buff), split winter redbud shoots (reddish), willow shoots (foundation)
H. 14⅞" Diam. 26⅛"
The Grace Hudson Museum, City of Ukiah

This style of storage basket is not only among the largest baskets traditionally made by the Pomo, but it is also completely covered with latticework, which is somewhat unusual. No doubt it was a special piece in the eyes of the weaver and the community.

Pomo weavers made large, globular, plain-twined baskets to hold any number of items in their homes: acorns, other baskets, clothes, anything that needed to be stored. Such baskets have been referred to as "dowry baskets." John Hudson, a noted ethnologist who lived in the Ukiah area around the turn of the century, explained that the basket was given to the new groom by his mother-in-law "or nearest relative of the bride" (Culin, 1907:111). In the Potter Valley Pomo language, the basket was called *chimo* (literally, "son-in-law").

Because of its size and the weight it might contain, some Pomo storage baskets were generally strengthened with a series of horizontal "lattice" bands incorporated into the weave. Often these one- or two-inch bands were spaced throughout the basket. An interesting feature of Pomo basketry is the "dau," a break in the pattern. Here it is seen in the widest design band, with the insertion of a different design motif. Although the reason for this intentional change in the pattern is not entirely understood, it often has been interpreted as a place where the spirit could come and go, to enter and inspect the basket or escape when the basket is destroyed (McLendon and Holland, 1979:115).

In 1907, when Stewart Culin collected a nearly identical basket for the Brooklyn Museum, Jennie Miller (also known as Polly Miller), who was from Potter Valley in Mendocino County, was probably one of only two weavers in the area who were still making such baskets.

Frank Tuttle: "This basket is just so large and so beautiful in its form, its shape and consistency, that it's inspiring. Whenever I see this type of basket, the lattice-twined basket, I'm always in awe—because it's unique. And I know how much work it takes to produce such a basket. Underneath every row there is a stick, and that stick had to be prepared, and all the weavers [weft strands], light and dark, had to be prepared; and then they had to be held in place, held with firm intention from top to bottom, from beginning to end. It just makes it an amazing object. And it's a strong basket. Technically, in terms of its use, its strength is something that needs to be appreciated. It's a very hidden but much appreciated quality of the basket. Visually it's very set, it's very stable and very static. In relationship to the human body it's such a nice shape. You have to kind of look around it. It asserts itself into your space when you're trying to hold it and carry it.

"The light and dark bands are real even. In this kind of basket, as in the sifters, the lattice bands are something I admire about the Pomo baskets. There's a consistency that seems to be achieved with a difficult technique and a complex design. There seems to be an evenness that the weaver strives for. There's a real balance there. It's all even. And that evenness allows for the complex design to show itself in a technique that doesn't readily lend itself to readability, to legibility in terms of the design. In this basket there's a real balance between large, dark triangular background shapes and these zigzagging light bands with small triangular motifs moving through them. And it's hard to see. It must have been an incredible process to make that happen. Our eye switches back and forth from these dark bands with designs to the restful plain bands where we just notice the texture of the surface.

"The design at the top has these large diamond shapes that aren't touching; there's a sizable distance between them. It allows them to be static and rest in place. Whereas that sort of gartersnake design in the middle moves in a very rapid zigzag, active pattern around this upper center. And then in the design below that, there's a reverse; light and dark, light and dark of a vertical pattern. For my eye, that light and dark in that particular band lends itself to the shape, in that the light part of the motif acts as a reflected light. Because when an object is turning up away from the surface it's sitting on, there's a reflected light underneath. And so the surface at that point would be lighter, it would be brighter. It would catch this bouncing light. And whether or not that's an intention of the weaver, for me as a painter, that's something I notice about it. It allows our eye and the basket—the bulge, the belly part of the basket—to move up to the rim, to the border. It uplifts that part of it.

"It's something that I like to point out to people who aren't aware of the technique. The texture that it offers us on the outside is quite different from the texture on the inside. So that's always a nice surprise."

Sherrie Smith-Ferri: "The way I usually think of these baskets is basically they're two baskets: one, the inside, is a twined basket; and the other, the outside, is a coiled basket; and they're sort of melded together. You've got foundation rods running horizontally and foundation rods running vertically, which makes it a very strong basket. It's reinforced. One of the things I always like about this close lattice-twined work is the diffuse appearance of the pattern. Because the design material, the colored weavers, aren't right next to each other. There's a space in between where you can see that sort of foundation rod coming through. Which gives it a kind of diffuse, misty quality. There are no real sharp lines, it's more suggestive. And I think it's very elegant."

Frank Tuttle: "I see those patterns that you're talking about, I hadn't really noticed that before. Because there's a verticality."

Sherrie Smith-Ferri: "Almost like columns. The other thing I was noticing is that whoever the weaver was, it looks like she was working two rows at the same time, which seems counterintuitive. It seems like that would be more difficult."

Frank Tuttle: "You would cover ground faster that way if you could do it."

Sherrie Smith-Ferri: "It's quite a technical feat, I would think, to be able to whip those guys along at the same time."

Frank Tuttle: "Yes, because you'd have two long sticks, two very long sticks. Then you'd have four sets of weavers, right?"

Sherrie Smith-Ferri: "Then you'd have your foundation rods running up the other way that you're manipulating too."

Frank Tuttle: "But then to keep your design going though. It sort of boggles my mind at the moment." [laughter]

Sherrie Smith-Ferri: "The other thing that's important to mention about these baskets is how much material it takes to do that close latticework versus just doing a plain twined basket. There's a lot of time and careful preparation of materials involved in producing this."

Frank Tuttle: "Those weavers are paper thin . . . . there's really nothing there but the color [redbud]."

Jenny Miller, Photograph by A.O. Carpenter. Courtesy of The Grace Hudson Museum, City of Ukiah.

Artist Unknown (Pomo)
STORAGE BASKET
c. 1905

willow shoots, split willow root
H. 9½" Diam. 15½"
The Oakland Museum of California

Strong small- and medium-sized lattice-twined baskets such as this were used by the Pomo as storage containers for the interior of houses. Willow shoots are gathered, stripped of their bark, and then stored for several months to completely dry or cure. When construction begins on the basket, the willow shoots are moistened to make them pliable.

During and after the gathering process, materials are painstakingly sorted. In a basket such as this, where the structure is so evident, one can see the near-perfect matching of sticks—the result of conscious sorting and a discriminating eye for detail.

Brian Tripp: "Very incredible!"

Frank LaPena: "The materials themselves give you the sense of what the form is and how they have been manipulated."

Judith Polanich: "It's gorgeous. The perfect shape and the minimalist quality are like the "bones" of a basket. That's always underneath, but with the close-twined baskets it's covered up. Here it's revealed. Completely successful."

L. Frank Manriquez: "Sometimes when you're taking photographs, you use black-and-white film so you won't be fooled by the color. You can appreciate composition and form. That's what this one does for me. It's real clean."

Frank Tuttle: "What I enjoy about this piece is that the lattice, the rib, asserts itself more than in the others. You see the ribs, you're faced with the ribs. The horizontal quality of the rib being there, that's the *ti* (the lattice), that's what it's about. The regularity of all the ribs, of all the sticks, catches the light. Those *ti's* are going to play a kind of shadow game. In large lattice-twined baskets the sticks take on a wirelike quality, they take on a metallic patina. They become something other than just sticks."

Vivien Hailstone: "I think this is a perfect basket. To make the rings around it that firm and that even is really a piece of art."

Sherrie Smith-Ferri: "That's the thing about this kind of basket. The material is so perfect and there's nothing to take away from that. You really realize how careful the weaver was in sizing and collecting those sticks."

Brian Tripp: "That's one of the things underlying our appreciation. This basket here is so plain and simple. But you can go all the way from this style clear up to one of these other baskets that's covered with feathers and beads. And in between you can see a whole wide range of baskets. This is the foundation, and even the foundation is beautiful."

Ella Johnson (Yurok) 1900–1990
TOBACCO BASKET
1955

split conifer root (buff), bear grass (white) woodwardia fern stem dyed with alder bark (rust),
maidenhair fern stem (black), willow shoots (foundation), buckskin
H. 7⅜" Diam. 7¼"
Collection of Albert Hailstone

Ella Steve Johnson was born in the ancient Yurok village of Weitchpec, which is on the Klamath River near its convergence with the Trinity River. She began weaving at the age of nine and continued to make a variety of Yurok baskets throughout her life. She played an important role in passing on the knowledge of Yurok weaving to a new generation when she taught classes at College of the Redwoods and for the Mainstream Program in Humboldt County during the 1970s. In 1974 Ella Johnson demonstrated her skills at the Smithsonian Institution's Folklife Festival in Washington, D.C.

The Yurok and Karuk people of the Klamath River region traditionally smoked tobacco in pipes. They raised their tobacco in tended gardens to be harvested and dried. Tobacco was stored in somewhat globular baskets, which were made with a lid that was attached with cordage or buckskin. A great many of the old tobacco baskets utilized one of two very conservative design ideas executed in bear grass overlay on conifer root. Both involve the alternating of grass and root, but one is an alternating vertical bar pattern covering the entire surface of the basket, and the other is a checkered pattern, sometimes referred to as a "salt and pepper" look. Ella Johnson combined both of these ideas in a limited, spaced, stair-stepped layout.

Vivien Hailstone: "Old-time tobacco pouches were made with simple designs. And mainly made with pine root. It's a good shape for an old-time tobacco pouch."

Brian Tripp: "The lid looks like it fits real nice."

Kathy Wallace: "Ella's work was an inspiration to my teachers. I'm privileged to have a cap she made for me. I also have a medallion she gave me when she found that I was starting to make baskets. It still inspires my work today. We're lucky she was so generous with her knowledge."

Ella Johnson, c. 1975. Courtesy of Mrs. Lillian Hostler.

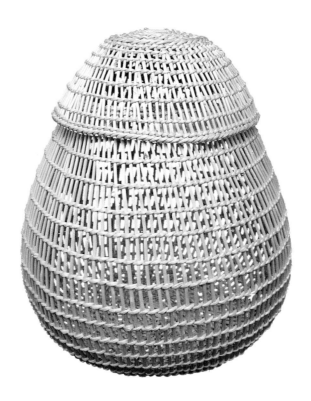

Loren Bommelyn (Tolowa/Karuk) 1956–
HERB STORAGE BASKET
1994

hazel shoots
H. 7¼" Diam. 7½"
Courtesy of the artist

While women created the vast majority of native basketry, men traditionally wove certain basket types, including many of the open-work, whole-shoot baskets. The manipulation of whole shoots, especially hazel shoots, requires a certain amount of hand strength, an attribute most women ascribe to men.

Loren not only makes baskets, but he is also a ceremonial leader in his community, a master of traditional Tolowa song, and a regalia maker. A fluent speaker of the Tolowa language, which he has taught for several years at Del Norte High School, he is currently pursuing a degree in linguistics at the University of Oregon. Loren made his first basket at age twelve. Since that time he has become one of the most respected makers of baby cradles and open-work twined workbaskets in northwestern California.

Loren is especially renowned for his meticulous attention to the evenness of the size of his materials when he is gathering and sorting his sticks. The symmetry and evenness of the weave evident in the finished basket is attributable to his strict selection process.

"There's a fancy part of the basket and a realistic part," says Loren. "You want to strive for perfection, but at the same time you want to make it for a function. You have to balance the two; the character of making it right and pretty and the character of making it for a use. I want my baskets to be used. The old Indians say that things like to be used, that when they aren't used they get lonesome." Loren also comments on the emotional investment that goes into a basket. "It's like I'm in love with every basket that I make. After it's made, I have to just sit there and look at it for a really long time. I wish I had old-timers around to critique me. I'd love to have someone tell me how to do it a different way, give me a new level to strive for.". (Mendelsohn, 1983:59-60)

Frank Tuttle: "What I enjoy about Loren's pieces is simply the overall uniformity. That means a considerable amount of attention paid to gathering, curing, and sorting his materials, as well as a commitment to an exacting weaving technique. First the whole grading part of it: he makes sure he has all of his sticks, more than enough, the same size. And then he's able to produce a basket like this, with that same uniformity, with such rapidity. What he's looking for is a container, the containment of volume; but equally, one senses the heartfelt adherence to a tradition of being in the right time and space. Everything has to be just right."

Kathy Wallace: "Having worked on an openwork all-stick basket this summer, I really appreciate his control. All of his twining across is so even, each stitch is so evenly done. I've watched him work, and he's got the strength in his hands to control the sticks. Although it's actually many sticks, and the sticks do taper quite a bit, it looks like he used one continuous weaver. For me, it was really hard because I didn't have the strength in my hands to keep it so even all the way around. So I really appreciate his work."

Loren Bommelyn, 1990. Photograph by John Bishop.

COOKING, SOUP
AND FEASTING
BASKETS

Artist Unknown (Yokuts)
COOKING BASKET
c. 1900

split sedge root (buff), split winter redbud shoots (reddish), dyed bracken root (black), deer grass stalks (foundation)
H. 8½" Diam. 17¼"
The Southwest Museum, Los Angeles

Yokuts is a generalized term that has been used historically to identify some forty linguistically related groups whose homeland included nearly all of the San Joaquin Valley, extending into the southern Sierra foothill regions of Mariposa, Madera, and Tulare Counties. It is unknown from which specific group this basket derived.

Yokuts people used large finely coiled baskets for making acorn soup and other foods. Like other native people throughout California, they cooked in baskets using the stone boiling method, in which two or three fire-heated stones are set in a basket containing leached acorn dough in water. The red hot stones are moved around, so that the basket is not seriously scorched or burned. This is an exceptionally finely woven cooking basket, with approximately 230 weft strands per square inch.

The three design bands in this basket repeat a motif found in a large number of Yokuts coiled wares, the very popular rattlesnake motif.

About snakes and baskets, Barbara Bill (Mono/Yokuts) said in 1991, "I remember when I went [gathering] with [my grandmother] she would pray, and then she would talk to the snake and say in her dialect, 'I'm coming to gather sticks. I'm not bothering you, and please don't bother me'." (Ortiz, 1991/1992: 24)

Judith Polanich: "Absolutely lapidary."

Craig Bates: "There's no doubt that the weaver of this basket was a master. It's an unusual idea to reverse colors; to change the top two bands and leave the bottom band like it's usually executed."

Judith Polanich: "With black on the outside and red on the inside?"

Craig Bates: "And then to make the starting and ending rows on the other two bands black when you've got the outside red and the inside black."

Frank LaPena: "I like the switch because from an aesthetic point of view the difference on the bottom, that lightness, the diamond lightness, lets it hold its own in relation to the others. And I like that. The others are getting bigger and taking more space, but the brightness of the smaller gives it more balance."

Judith Polanich: "It's difficult when you're using bands like this to get variation while still maintaining that same sort of very restrained quality. It's a nice basket."

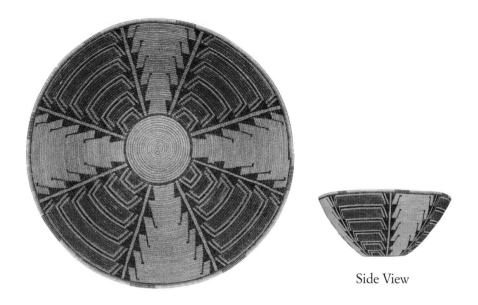

Side View

Artist Unknown (Shoshone)
COOKING OR MIXING BASKET
c. 1900

split willow shoots (buff), split devil's claw (black), Joshua tree root (red), willow shoots (foundation)
H. 5⅝" Diam. 13¾"
State of California, Department of Parks and Recreation

Shoshone-speaking peoples have occupied the vast spaces of Nevada, and parts of Utah, Idaho, and eastern California— a region known as the Great Basin—for thousands of years. It is an area where most Shoshone still live. The region in and around Death Valley and the Panamint Mountains served as home for some remarkable basketmakers. The three-rod coiled basketry produced there around the turn of the century is thought by many to be among the world's finest.

While the form of this basket suggests a traditional boiling or mixing bowl, it is unlikely that this piece was ever used, more likely having been made for market sale. The four vertical polychrome design bands on this basket show strong affiliation to popular motifs used among the Tubatulabal and Yokuts of the southern San Joaquin Valley, an example of the movement and adaptation of design ideas and basket forms that has occurred throughout western basketry traditions.

Frank LaPena: "This motif is really nice because of the way it shows that design element from those earlier pieces being manipulated in another fashion."

Judith Polanich: "One of the interesting things about these southern Sierra designs is the way they cope with the curve of the wall. All over California, people have different strategies for these adjustments, but here, as the diameter of the basket grows, and the weavers need to make the pattern wider, they're busy counting out those little triangles and they don't have the flexibility to expand that part of the design. They're so intent on building triangles systematically that they make adjustments in the negative space or in the column, a sort of red negative space."

Denise Davis: "Four patterns are hard, too, much harder than three. I was told that specifically. Five's easier, three's easier, but four is really, really difficult. It is a balance, the white and the dark. And the way it's executed in this basket is just beautiful, because that is hard work."

Mary Tecuyas (Tubatulabal?) c. 1810–c. 1916
COOKING BASKET
c. 1890

split sumac shoots (white), Joshua tree root (red), dyed bracken root (black), deer grass stalks (foundation)
H. 8⅜" Diam. 18¾"
The Field Museum of Natural History

The Tubatulabal homeland incorporates much of the Kern River drainage from its source in the southern Sierra to its entry into the southern San Joaquin Valley. Mary Tecuyas and her family were residing at Fort Tejon when this basket was collected.

This basket was originally acquired by E.L. McCleod and appears in the historic publication, *American Indian Basketry*, by Otis Mason. Some of the small isolated design elements are quite similar to those incorporated by Yokuts weavers to the north and west, and the Shoshone to the east. The red hourglass shape outlined with black has often been referred to as a butterfly motif. The small motif of four joined rectangles found directly below this is identified as "flies." Another pattern farther down the basket, a design made up of six connecting rectangles, is similar to a motif the Yokuts called "water skater."

Frank LaPena: "That's real nice. It's real strong. The whole movement set off by the little dark areas is so powerful, has such presence, because of the five dark jagged forms radiating toward the center. You're obviously going to be dragged into it. But then the little dark outline on the edge catches your attention. And bold as it is, it almost makes it more subtle. I'm not quite sure. When I look at this basket, I see the small individual designs all playing around it as if it were flat, revolving around the center; and what the [edge designs] do is keep that energy from moving through it. Maybe by creating the real excitement that is obviously there. They go from small to larger, and it all evens out, and then I have to look at the whole thing."

Brian Tripp: "Very airy. I like the way those little elements are placed, with the big zigzag floating around through them."

Brian Bibby: "What do you think makes this piece successful?"

Brian Tripp: "The action, the movement. They way the spiral goes around and connects to that black circle in the center. The outlining of the red zigzag with black is real nice, too."

L. Frank Manriquez: "Plus there's a vortex going on, really dragging you in. The design forces movement. The smaller design elements are traveling at a different speed than the larger design, causing motion."

Frank Tuttle: "Those little center motifs, as small and delicate as they are, and that vortex, they're in horizontal movement, all swirling and emphasizing the funnel effect."

Artist Unknown (Pomo)
COOKING BASKET
c. 1895

split sedge root (buff), split winter redbud shoots (reddish), willow shoots? (foundation)
H. 9½" Diam. 15"
State of California, Department of Parks and Recreation

Although Pomoan peoples are largely known for their fine coiled basketry, most of the baskets they used for gathering, cooking, and processing foods were made using one or more of seven different twining techniques. In this diagonally twined basket, the remarkably flat smooth surface and graceful shape are a testament to the masterful control this weaver had over her materials.

Judith Polanich: "This is a basket that reminds me of one of the first things that attracted me to California basketry. It's just like a soap bubble: it's so thin, it's so fine, it encloses such a large space, but you could hold it on three fingers. Magical."

Frank LaPena: "The design is strong—the black and white going through it. The design creates a boldness that really holds you. It's riveting."

Artist Unknown (Yurok/Karuk/Hupa)
COOKING BASKET
c. 1900

split conifer root (buff), bear grass (white), hazel shoots? (foundation)
H. 10½" Diam. 14⅜"
State of California, Department of Parks and Recreation

Cooking baskets from the Klamath River region are traditionally twined of pine root with a single horizontal band of bear grass overlay on the upper portion of the basket. Some weavers believe the placement of the design band is strategic, keeping it away from the part of the basket that is exposed to the most heat and moisture in the cooking process. It is interesting to note that when a cooking basket has been used for some time, or when it is wet and in use, the conifer root area becomes darker so that the contrast with the bear grass is greater.

Vivien Hailstone: "For cooking baskets we usually use hazel sticks and only root and bear grass overlay. The black maidenhair fern is not strong enough. Bear grass is tough and it can stand more heat. The ridge around the basket is formed from two large roots wrapped around the middle part of the basket to make it stronger."

Kathy Wallace: "I remember my grandma, Geneva Risling, cooking acorn mush in a basket like this when her old friend Suzie Little came to visit. Suzie didn't like the taste that metal pots gave the acorn. So only mush cooked with rocks in a basket were served to her. They'd sit and laugh and speak to each other in Yurok. The acorn mush that stuck to the cooking rocks was given to people as a special treat."

Lori Smith: "This thing is perfect. The weave is so consistent. This is really nice."

Brian Bibby: "Why is it nice? What makes it nice?"

Lori Smith: "All the materials are precisely same size; the roots, the sticks. The shape—it's so straight, up and down. It's tightly woven. It's built heavy enough to be used, but somebody took the time to do it right. This is what I would call a perfect basket."

Lori Smith (Yurok/Wailaki) 1961–

SOUP BASKET
1995

split spruce root (buff), bear grass (white), willow shoots (foundation)
H. 3⅛" Diam. 6¼"
Collection of the artist

The Yurok mush or soup basket is nearly identical to the cooking basket in materials (conifer root field with bear grass figure) and design (a horizontally arranged pattern on the upper third of the basket), except that the soup basket is smaller in size. A few documented examples suggest that cooking and soup bowls may have been made in sets carrying the same design patterns. Traditionally, this basket would have been used primarily as an individual food bowl, mainly for acorn soup.

Lori Smith, born in Fortuna and raised in the Ferndale area, felt an early interest in traditional Yurok basketry: "I was always curious about baskets because we had two baskets that my great-great grandmother wove. I realized at a very young age no one was doing this work. It was a part of my culture that was lost, really, because nobody in my family knew how to do it. There were no women left in that generation, in my immediate family, that were basketweavers. So it took until I was twenty-seven until I found somebody [Yurok elder Vera Ryerson] to teach me.

"I've always been kind of a perfectionist. Some of my first glimpses of baskets were from Lizzie Hickox [see page 95]. I would look at those types of baskets in the museum, and it's like. . .whoa! I've got a long ways to go. And I didn't realize that not everybody wove that fine. So I just worked and worked and worked. So now I think I'm finally getting to that stage. I cranked out a lot of little miniature baskets and didn't spend time doing a big basket until I perfected my weave. For one thing I didn't want to waste materials. They're too hard to get and too time-consuming.

"So the mush bowl is my first big piece. And it hasn't been shaped either. Some people, after they weave the basket they have to stuff it to make the bottom just so, but that is its original, natural shape. To me it's almost like being a potter, how you're

Lori Smith, 1995. Photograph by Dugan Aguilar.

shaping it with your hands. If I see it flaring out a little bit too much or I want to start going in a little bit more, I just slowly pull that stick in as I tighten it. Then you slowly do it on the next row and the next row and then you get the real gradual tightening."

Lori said she made this old-style basket because she felt too few of them were being made. And the soup basket materials appeal to her: "After weaving with all the materials that I can weave with, including porcupine quills, bear grass and spruce root are my favorites. The color combination and everything else about it, I'm just attracted to it. I've always woven with spruce root. That's what I learned with and that's what I like. It's what I have a feel for. I've tried pine [root] and I don't like it. Spruce really complements the bear grass and vice versa. They just kind of go together, like bread and butter."

The design or "mark" Lori used in this bowl is known as "sturgeon back" among the Yurok. In discussing her choice of this mark for her basket, Lori described the way she plans her weaving: "Sometimes I spend a week figuring out a design, and I have to have all that in my head before I start counting off my sticks.

Once I start a basket, I can hardly put it down. I've caught myself staying up until three-thirty in the morning, especially once that design starts going in. Once I get that design in, it's like I'm connected with it and I can't quit until it's done. It's just that fulfillment of seeing the finished product, I guess." (Lori Smith, 1996)

Artist Unknown (Konkow)
FEASTING BASKET
c. 1900

split shoots (buff), split winter redbud shoots (reddish), willow shoots (foundation)
H. 19½" Diam. 29½"
State of California, Department of Parks and Recreation, Bidwell Mansion State Historic Park

Baskets shaped like traditional cooking baskets but much larger were used at important gatherings and ceremonial occasions to serve acorn soup and possibly other foods. The soup would be cooked in the normal-sized baskets and then poured into these magnificent feasting vessels. One historical photograph shows that four men and an encircling rope were needed to carry such a feasting basket full of acorn soup.

The Konkow living in the upper Sacramento Valley often had occasion for using these large baskets as their year was filled with a series of ceremonial dances. From early fall through late spring, ceremonial performances occurred about every three to four weeks. Certain women were responsible for preparing and cooking food at such ceremonial events. This involved a great deal of work, but it was also a prestigious position in the community. Generally the wealthier families in the village sponsored the dance and provided much of the food, the labor, and the fine large tureens that held the acorn soup and other foods.

Although many Konkow were forced onto the Round Valley Reservation in Mendocino County by federal troops in 1863 and several Konkow families have remained there, their original homeland of Butte County currently has four federally recognized Konkow communities.

Craig Bates: "This is the basket that Henry Azbill, who was from the village at Chico, thought was made by Polly Slack. He said its design and shape were just like the one she made for her husband's memorial burning. She labored for four years on that basket. When she completed it, they had to take the wall out of her house in order to get it out."

Denise Davis: "The edges on this basket are so amazing. Every once in a while you'll see an old basket like this and it has such a wonderful edge, absolutely perfect. It doesn't skip a beat. That rhythm . . . she's got it. These women had a way. It's almost perfection, with that rhythm they're creating in the form through the design. And so straight, so precise . . . it's exciting. I look at this basket and think, boy, this person had a wonderful life. They were such artists, such talented women.

"And I love to look at these baskets sideways. I always look at the rows and how smooth they are. Some baskets you can see each ridge and they actually bulge out. The ones that are as smooth as this and have that edge, you know, that's really hard. It takes flawless control."

CAPS AND CRADLES

Artist Unknown (Modoc/Klamath)
WOMAN'S CAP
c. 1895

split phragmites stems (buff), dyed tule (black), twisted tule stems (foundation), porcupine quills dyed with wolf moss (yellow), nettle fiber cordage (gray)
H. 4½" Diam. 8"
The Southwest Museum, Los Angeles

The Modoc formerly lived in an area of northeastern California and southern Oregon. After the war of 1872 which took place in the lava beds near Tule Lake, many Modoc were exiled to Indian Territory in Oklahoma. By 1900 some had returned to live in southern Oregon communities with those Modoc who had remained.

Modoc and Klamath caps are quite flexible because their foundations are made from twisted tule rather than the woody shoots used in most other twined ware in California. The dark design motif is carried out with tule that has been dyed in a dark iron-rich mud. Similar caps were made by the Achumawi to the south, the Umatilla and Cayuse of eastern Washington and Oregon, and the Nez Perce in Idaho.

Frank LaPena: "What's really nice here is the use of the quills as a running line. And the addition of color adds a richness to the design."

Artist Unknown (Owens Valley Paiute)
WOMAN'S CAP
c. 1900

split willow shoots (white and black), willow shoots (foundation)
H. 4¾" Diam. 8⅞"
Phoebe A. Hearst Museum of Anthropology, University of California, Berkeley

The Owens Valley is located at the base of the Eastern Sierra. It stretches some eighty miles and includes contemporary Paiute communities in Bishop, Lone Pine, Big Pine, and Independence. This area between Mono Lake and the formerly great inland body of water, Owens Lake, was once described as an "amply watered glen," fed by runoff from the Sierra. The Owens River traverses the length of the valley and functions much like an aorta, serving as the central waterway that pumps life into an otherwise arid environment. Traditionally, the Owens Valley Paiute practiced artificial irrigation by forcing water to flood specific areas in order to create a more advantageous environment for certain bulbs and tubers that were among their important food crops.

The Owens Valley Paiute utilized more than forty plants for food. Even with their abundant water resources, they had to be highly migratory in order to successfully exploit seasonal food and other resources that occurred in different micro-environments, often many miles apart. This kind of movement may have favored the development of basketry, since light and sturdy baskets have quite an advantage over other alternatives, such as pottery or metalware.

Among the most important food crops gathered in this migratory cycle were the nuts of the piñon pine. In the fall of the year the Paiute would set up camps in the hill regions bordering the Owens Valley. Groups might stay for several weeks to harvest the sticky pine cones, extract the nuts, and perhaps parch the meats for winter storage.

Craig Bates: "There were a great number of these caps collected around 1900, but they became much less common after that. One thing I've noticed about several of the ones I've looked at from Owens Valley is that the start, the first row of twining, will sometimes be done with twisted sinew cordage."

Judith Polanich: "This basket is made with 'winter-peeled' willow, that is, willow peeled in the winter when the dark underskin adheres and doesn't come off. The pattern is made by turning the material over, with the dark part out for the dark, and the light side of the strand out for the white. This has been overpainted, but just in the patterned band; they make the dark side darker by painting with black and the white whiter by painting with white, which is how they heighten the contrast."

Craig Bates: "There's an inherent problem with doing diagonal twining that way. The rounded side that has the thin bark stuck on it is covering the cambium layer, or the sapwood, so that doesn't pick up dirt. That's why when you trim the width of the sewing strands on a basket, you always trim from the back to make it smooth, because that's the rougher, split side. But when you turn that and have the flat, split face turning out, that's the side that picks up dirt."

Judith Polanich: "So if you really want to do it right and what you want to do is to heighten the contrast to make the pattern bolder, paint is a good solution. In Owens Valley they used white clay, and a black dye made from a couple of different recipes."

Craig Bates: "Boiled ephedra and yellow ochre are another recipe for staining the inner bark."

Judith Polanich: "If you're going to carry weight on your back with a tumpline, you don't want it chafing your forehead. Throughout California, caps are worn to prevent that. That's part of the purpose they serve in Owens Valley, but the Paiute caps are bigger than the ones in northern California. They fit over the head kind of like a rain hat. In some field notes, I've found discussions of women wrapping their hair up and putting it on top of their heads underneath these hats. Apparently the women wore these caps for gathering piñon nuts and that hairdo prevented the piñon pitch from getting in their hair. So that might explain the broader hat: protection from the sun and piñon pitch as well as from chafing."

Craig Bates: "This style of cap represents the finest example of Paiute twining ever produced. It's so thin-walled."

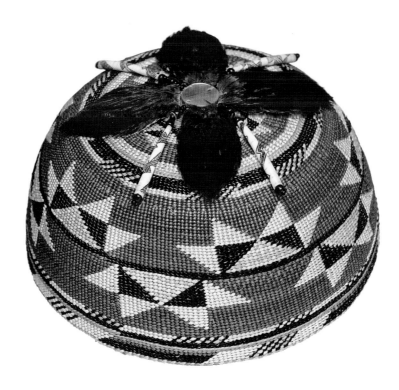

Amy Smoker (Yurok) 1897–1989

WOMAN'S CEREMONIAL CAP
c. 1948

willow root (buff), bear grass (white), woodwardia fern stem dyed with alder bark (rust), maidenhair fern stem (black),
porcupine quill dyed with staghorn lichen (yellow), willow shoots (foundation),
pileated woodpecker scalps, dentalia shell, abalone shell
H. 3½" Diam. 7⅜"
Collection of Vivien Hailstone

Amy Smoker was born in Kepel, an ancient Yurok village that was site of a famous Yurok fish dam and the "first salmon" rites. As a weaver she was respected throughout the Klamath River region. Her repertoire included highly ornamental tobacco baskets, miniatures, gift baskets, baby cradles, fruit baskets, and caps. Mrs. Smoker said that she preferred "to do the fine work rather than the open-work baskets," (Kelsey, 1975) and her caps reveal her skill in this style. Their shape, the layout of the motifs, and her excellent technique distinguish her caps as among the finest of her day.

Ceremonial caps such as this one are usually used by young women who have yet to bear children. The caps—often lavishly ornamented with the rarest and most valuable gifts of nature such as woodpecker scalps and dentalia shells—enhance the stunning display of the ceremonial dances, during which some two dozen girls might parade into the rectangular, semisubterranean dance pit, interlock arms with male dancers, and gracefully bob up and down on the balls of their feet in rhythm with the singing.

Judith Polanich: "With the woodpecker scalps and the dentalia shells, this looks very special."

Vivien Hailstone: "I decorated it myself. This is how you decorate the hats for the ceremony (Brush Dance). When you go to the dances, you see that they decorate the hats used in ceremonies now."

Brian Tripp: "This is one of those baskets where the design is perfect. It just sparkles. The black just kind of bounces around with that black ring. Of course, with all the design this cap's got on it, all the embellishment, you can't imagine this cap without all that now."

Vivien Hailstone: "It's made correctly. This is the correct way to make a hat."

Kathy Wallace: "There are three distinct areas in making a cap: there's the top, there's the part that comes down the side, and there's the rim. It's made to fit the measurements of the person who is going to wear the cap. It's measured from the tip of her finger to the first knuckle, that's the first circle. Then from the tip of the finger to the bottom knuckle, that's where the rim starts; and then the thumbnail width (for the rim design area). To find out if it's the right size you have the person who's going to wear the cap open her hand inside it: if she can touch [the edges], it's the right size. I'm told you make caps a little bit bigger now because of curly hair. The cap isn't tried on until it's all finished, so that's how the weaver measures it.

"So there are three distinct bands that you won't find on any other baskets, you only find them on caps. Caps have the design on the top, not like a bowl, which would be plain on the bottom with the design starting on the side after the bowl turns upward. And these caps are for dances, so you've got to realize that our dance pits are subterranean, and the people watching the dance look down. That's why you want that top decorated, because you look down on the girls dancing. You can look down and see the tops of their caps."

Amy Smoker, c. 1980. Courtesy of Clarke Memorial Museum.

Ada Charles (Yurok) 1909 –
WOMAN'S CAP
c. 1965

willow root (interior weft), bear grass (white), maidenhair fern stem (black), willow shoots (foundation)
H. 3½" Diam. 7"
Collection of Herb and Peggy Puffer

Ada Charles, who now lives in Klamath, California, was born in the historic Yurok town of Wokel on the lower Klamath River. She began making baskets at age five under the tutelage of her mother. She is adept at making numerous types of traditional Yurok baskets, including cooking, wood-gathering, and storage baskets, as well as innovative pieces, such as woven hair-ties, table mats, earrings, and medallion necklaces. When asked about her basketmaking, Mrs. Charles once said, "I make baskets for pleasure and also I make baskets to use around the house. I make a baby basket each time a grandchild is born. I like to make baskets. Sometimes when I go someplace, I can hardly wait to get home so I can get started making baskets again." (Kelsey, 1975) Among the many baskets Mrs. Charles has made are scores of caps, primarily woven for native people.

Caps have a special character in Yurok society, as was noted by ethnographer Lila M. O'Neale: "A cap represents even today a choice possession, and a weaver's ability to make a good one will give her a widespread reputation as an expert. . . . Caps have always had a sale value among the Indians themselves, above that of any other type of basket. Into them, as everybody knew, went the most carefully selected materials and the best workmanship." (O'Neale, 1932:43)

Even a relatively small basket such as this cap requires the selection and preparation of an astonishing amount of material. The finished materials used in this one piece include:

split willow root, 225 linear feet

bear grass, 118 linear feet

maidenhair fern, 82 linear feet

willow sticks, 81 linear feet.

Laid end to end, this material would cover one and two-thirds football fields, or be about the height of a forty-story building. It is not simply the materials, but the weaving skills that are admired in a fine cap, as O'Neale notes: "Younger women bought [caps] from older weavers with reputations for fine work. . . ." Indeed, this cap had been bought around 1965 by Karuk basketmaker Florence Harry for her own use.

Kathy Wallace: "[I used to hear that] if you make a cap that has lots of holes and is too loose, your children will be stupid, because all their brains will fall through the holes.

"Caps like this one would really show up. The ceremonial dances are often viewed at night, from a distance; the bold black-and-white design on this cap would make it stand out, even at a distance, even in the dark."

Artist Unknown (Kawaiisu)
WOMAN'S CAP
c. 1900

split willow shoots (white), Joshua tree root (red), split devil's claw (black), deer grass (foundation)
H. 4½" Diam. 7½"
The Field Museum of Natural History

In addition to the wide distribution of twined basketry caps in northern California, Oregon, and the Great Basin, traditions of coiled caps existed in much of the south-central portion of the state, for example, among the Kawaiisu. The Kawaiisu homeland is located at the southern end of the Sierra Nevada range, below the Kern River drainage; it borders the Tehachapi mountains on the west and the Mojave Desert to the south and east. The environment is semi-arid, and vegetation can be sparse. Acorns from seven varieties of oaks were their major food resource. The Kawaiisu made the same array of baskets for collecting and processing foods as most other native peoples in California. That baskets were an important and valuable aspect of Kawaiisu culture is indicated by the first recorded meeting between the group and Europeans, in May of 1776, when Francisco Garces came upon a village and noted in his diary, "There were none but women and children who made us presents of meat, seeds and even of two baskets to take along with us." (Coues, 1900, 1:304-305)

Kawaiisu caps were worn only by women and sometimes doubled as personal food bowls. (Zigmond, 1978:205) Design layout and placement ideas for Kawaiisu caps appear to include two definite borders, often articulated by a single row of black at the crest where the basket begins to turn downward, and again a few rows from the selvage. The last two or three rows of the rim often include groups of black "ticking" as a finish design. The motif found in the main body of the present example is known to the Kawaiisu as, *ayataniit 'kad'*, referring to "butterfly." (Zigmond, 1978:207) This example was collected by Mrs. William Tevis from a weaver living near Caliente Creek in Kern County near the turn of the century.

Judith Polanich: "Hats are so interesting. I mean, the idea of hats. Look at this one, perfect, fine, colorful, beautifully thought out and executed. And all the literature says that women wore hats for protection from the tumpline, so you think, Aha, this is a practical art. But in other areas, like parts of southern California, their hats were not even decorated, just twined open-work juncus bowls. They must have worked as practical hats, but they're not like these. And whole vast regions of California with wonderful basketmakers, like the Pomo, didn't even bother with hats. Just think what a Pomo dress hat would have been like!

"If you go back to the idea of hat-making as a 'practical art', you have to remember that it's usually the fancy version that got saved. When women weave a dress hat, it's usually the finest weaving of all: tiny stitches, perfect materials, meticulous preparation, elegant layout, complex design, and virtuoso work. It goes far beyond what is required to be practical, far more 'art' than 'practical art'. So for every work hat, there's probably a hundred dress caps, because everybody saved the fancy ones, not the work ones. And those fancy ones aren't anything but art."

Frank LaPena: "The idea of having the running squares is really neat. The idea of the variation of the square design element, moving those shapes through that piece. I think it's interesting that there are four square elements and four diagonal patterns. I like that kind of abstract form: squares and rectangles. A square, that's not organic, but then the color and tone of the materials, the tan, red, and black: . . that makes it organic."

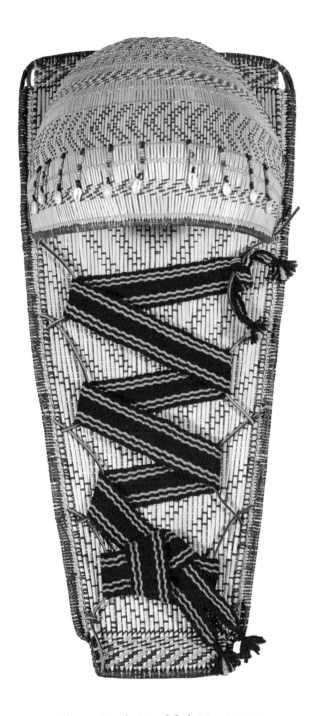

Ulysses Goode (Northfork Mono) 1927–

CRADLE BASKET
1984

sourberry shoots (cradle foundation), split winter redbud shoots (reddish), split sedge root (buff), deer brush shoots (hood), cowry shells, glass beads, yarn
H. 11½" L. 30¾" W. 14½" to 8"
Collection of Ron W. Goode and Myra Kirk-Goode

When he was a child, Uly saw his elder relatives making baskets every day. He showed an interest in their basketry at an early age and was initially given small basket "starts" to work on. Uly later learned that there were several men who had made basketry in the old days. Uly continues to collect and weave, living on his family property outside of Northfork in Madera County.

Uly is adept at making Western Mono style winnowing, burden, and coiled baskets, as well as cradles. When asked what he liked best about basketmaking Uly said: "Putting the basket together. It's the culmination of all your work. You see these sticks and stuff out there in the hills and then you've put this basket together." His reputation as a fine weaver may be attributable to the way he approaches the art. "With a basket I don't say, 'That's good enough'. The basket comes out right because I make it that way. I take pride in what I do."

Uly has made over four hundred cradles in the past twenty years. Uly and his late wife often worked on cradles together, with her making the back board and him making the hood. Uly draws from one of the four traditional Western Mono cradle patterns that he knows. The Western Mono weavers use different designs for girls and boys. The designs are executed in the dark winter redbud, on the back board and on the hood. For boys there is the diagonal line and the "arrow" design; for girls, a vertical zigzag and a crossing pattern. In addition to full-sized cradles like this one, Western Mono weavers sometimes make "receiving" cradles; intended for a newborn baby, the receiving cradle is somewhat smaller and usually does not contain sex-specific designs. The majority of Mr. Goode's cradles are still used within the native community.

Ulysses Goode, undated. Courtesy of Ron Goode.

Judith Polanich: "This basket is really quite complicated. It's actually three baskets in one: the back, the arch, and the hood are all made separately. It needs two different warp materials, two weft materials, and three different weaves. Uly is a great weaver and really articulate about weaving and what makes a good basket. He can explain what is critical to achieving the proper shape and how it's necessary for the function of the basket. I must have made my baby cradle three times; when the work wasn't just right, Uly would just wait until I realized that I had to undo it, and then show me again. He's very skilled at weaving all the Western Mono baskets.

Craig Bates: "This cradle couldn't have been made before 1978 or so. Initially it looks like it's completely an old-style cradle, but there are several important differences. The hood is covered with design, compared to older cradles. Those additional bands of redbud chevrons are a new idea for cradle hoods that I didn't see happening until at least the end of the 1970s. I don't remember them before then.

"Also, most of the time those bead and shell pendants are hung from the center of the bow, the center of the main chevron design on the hood. Until recently I'd never seen them hung from the bottom like that. And the use of cowry shells is a totally new, innovative thing. The older cradles tend to have fewer pendants and they're in groups of four, five, or six pendants together. So it's a good example of how this weaver has kept a traditional form for a cradle, but has modified it to make it distinctly his own."

CEREMONIAL
AND GIFT BASKETS

Artist Unknown (Yurok)
JUMP DANCE BASKET
c. 1920

split conifer root (interior weft), bear grass (white), maidenhair fern stem (black), willow shoots (foundation), buckskin, paint, eagle plume
L. 23½" W. 5" x 7½"
The Southwest Museum, Los Angeles

Every autumn the Yurok and their Karuk and Hupa neighbors hold a Jump Dance—a ten-day ceremony with a focus on "fixing" the world. This grand ceremony provides a stunning display of regalia, an integral part of which is this cylindrically shaped basket. Each male dancer holds such a basket in one hand and at certain moments of the dance, with a sweeping motion across the body, raises the basket skyward.

The Jump Dance basket is one of the more unusual examples of basketry in California; unlike nearly all other examples of twining, it is not made in a radial progression. Instead it is a rectangular woven mat that is rolled into a cylindrical shape when done. The ends are covered over with buckskin, and an open slit is formed where the mat meets, held in form by two wooden rods that are attached to each edge of the rolled mat by buckskin that has been sewn to incorporate basket and rod. The basket is made by women, but the geometric painting adorning the buckskin and the attachment of feathers is done by men.

Some say the basket's shape is significant, resembling as it does the elkhorn "purses" that have traditionally been used to hold items of wealth, such as dentalia shells, which are evidence of good luck and good standing with Spirit Beings known in Yurok as *woge*.

Brian Tripp: "A lot of times there are some bands that split the center of the design. I've heard this design called "crab claw." This is one of the few baskets that's totally ceremonial. The women made them, but the men used them. This painting on the end would have been done by a man.

Denise Davis: "The painting really complements the basket's form as a sculpture."

Yurok Jump Dance, c. 1900. Photograph by W. Ericson. Courtesy State of California, Department of Parks and Recreation.

Artist Unknown (Pomo)

GIFT BASKET
c. 1880

split sedge root (buff), split and dyed bulrush root (black), willow shoots (foundation), acorn woodpecker crest feathers,
valley quail topknots, clamshell disc beads, glass beads, cotton thread
H. 5¼" Diam. 7¾" x 9"
The Haggin Museum

Coiled, oval-shaped "canoe" baskets have sometimes been described as being made for "doctors," the shape of the basket being appropriate for storing or carrying their various rattles, medicines, and other paraphernalia. Examples range in size from baskets more than four feet long to miniatures of less than two inches.

The decorations on this basket are extraordinary. The brilliant scarlet crest feathers of the acorn woodpecker were nearly always reserved for a highly valued ceremonial or gift basket such as this. The small white glass trade beads must also have been valuable. These beads became available to the Pomo and other native peoples of northern California in the early nineteenth century. Basket-weavers soon began to use them as delicate highlights within dark design areas, sewing them onto the basket with cotton thread rather than weaving them into the foundation.

Disc beads were made from shells of the Washington clam, which was obtained on the coast. Typically, the men made these beads, breaking the shells into pieces, roughing them into a rounded form, and then drilling them, using a hand drill spun between the palms (later the pump drill). A group of these drilled discs was strung on wire grass or on slender shoot material and then rolled on a smooth, flat stone until all the beads were evenly rounded and of the same diameter. This was Pomo money, here attached to the rim of the basket and further ornamented with quail topknot feathers.

Craig Bates: "Sherrie, what do you think about the size of these boat-shaped baskets. Do they get bigger as time goes on?"

Sherrie Smith-Ferri: "There seem to be some really huge ones, like four or five feet long. One is pictured with a child sitting inside it, looking just like a real canoe. There seems, for some reason, to have been a big production of them around 1905. You don't see the huge boat baskets much after that, maybe because they were too much work. I've heard people say that the larger ones are more traditional because you could fit the doctoring stuff in them. Another thing I've heard is that when you add the quail plumes at the rim of the basket, where they're sewn under the clamshell disc beads, you always have four—four groupings around the rim. That's the right number to use."

Artist Unknown (Pomo)
GIFT BASKET
c. 1910

split sedge root (buff), dyed bulrush root (black), willow shoots (foundation), acorn woodpecker
crest feathers (red), valley quail topknots, clamshell disc beads
H. 6" Diam. 10⅞"
State of California, Department of Parks and Recreation

Among the Pomo, baskets of exceptionally fine weave that incorporated materials of great value (woodpecker crest feathers, clamshell money) became, themselves, symbols of wealth. They had roles in the exchanges of property that marked certain important personal and community events, such as young women's coming of age ceremonies, weddings, or any situation for which a valuable gift might be appropriate or a payment required. By the turn of the century, these Pomo "jewel baskets" were in great demand among non-Indian collectors who had no real use for traditional utilitarian baskets and acquired these ornamental baskets as objects of art. Considering the relatively short time span most of these baskets were collected (c. 1890–1915), they were produced in remarkable numbers. This example was collected from the Eastern Pomo at Kelseyville (Lake County) by C.P. Wilcomb.

Frank Tuttle: "What strikes me about this basket is its wideness."

Sherrie Smith-Ferri: "It doesn't really come in very much at the top."

Frank Tuttle: "Right. It just tips up very subtly. And for me, that wideness is based on the fact that the dark pattern is so even from top to bottom. It makes it flat, like wallpaper. The design element is not manipulated with a lot of contrast, like from small to medium to large, and so it adds to its boldness. From top to bottom there seems to be an almost straight-sided effect. And all those little woodpecker tufts in there [are] only on the light sides."

Sherrie Smith-Ferri: "It's a very definite way of making what you think of as the relief part of the pattern really come alive with color. [There is a] sculptural quality to the feathers projecting out of the face of the basket."

Frank Tuttle: "Yeah, because that's what it would be. It would be a slight velvet, a velour feeling. Because there's the solid surface of the basket, and then there's an airy, light-catching device, with all the little feathers sticking out. So you get hints of red triangles and black triangles, with that little step pattern going up and down, that crisscrossing."

Sherrie Smith-Ferri: "And then that really bright light rim of the clamshell beads, which really helps finish it. With the black and the white and the red all playing off each other."

Frank Tuttle: "And those little diagonal tufts going into the surface, they're somewhat perpendicular to the surface. The black sits on the surface and then the clamshells sit at the top and are so regular. It does just hold it right off."

Sherrie Smith-Ferri: "It really is nice to know what these baskets were supposed to look like. I see a lot of the old baskets that have the spot feathering, and the red feathers have been eaten away. You only see tiny holes where they used to be. It removes a whole dimension from the basket. It makes a difference when they're gone. The weaver was really working with them as a design element. They're not just an addition that was thrown on at the end, they were part of the whole conception and execution from beginning to end."

Frank Tuttle: "Yeah, she was very conscious of the material and how she manipulated it. And not only are the materials manipulated in such a way as to create such a unique and special object, but then the object demands something of its handlers, to hold it—because it would be fuzzy, there'd be a fuzziness to it. Knowing how careful one has to be with them, that adds another dimension to these baskets. A specialness, a uniqueness just goes along with them. It's important to know that the basic idea of baskets can go all the way from everyday, work-a-day knockabout, to something that sits and asks to be viewed."

Sherrie Smith-Ferri: "It's really sort of an heirloom piece."

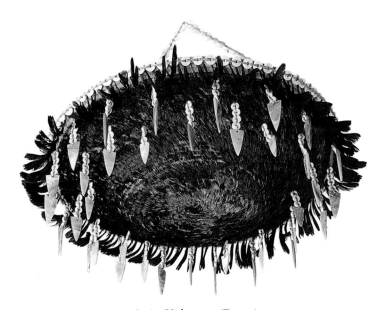

Artist Unknown (Pomo)
GIFT BASKET
c. 1900

split sedge root (buff), willow shoots (foundation), acorn woodpecker crest feathers (red), western bluebird crest feathers (blue),
mallard crest and neck feathers (green), valley quail topknots, clamshell disc beads, abalone shell
H. 1⅝" Diam. 9"
The Field Museum of Natural History

Fully feathered baskets were made in at least two general forms: closed forms, which are globular bowl-shaped baskets, often using mallard neck feathers for the color field; and open forms, which are generally larger, flaring bowl or tray-shaped baskets, often using valuable woodpecker crest feathers as the main color field. There are special techniques for working with feathers, especially the crest feathers of the acorn woodpecker, which are very small, only about three-eights of an inch in length. The weaver spins two or three of these tiny tufts between her thumb and forefinger to compact the quill ends together. She then places the tufts under the newest sewing stand of the basket, just before it is cinched tight. The weaver has to be careful of the angle of the tuft so that when it is cinched, its direction doesn't change. Often the weaver must do a significant amount of adjusting to make sure that all the tufts are lying at the correct angle and that the camber of the feathers is aligned. There is some evidence to suggest that in earlier times these display baskets were suspended from the ceiling area of Pomoan houses by the clamshell-laden string attached to the rim.

This basket was collected by Carl Purdy at Upper Lake. It was eventually purchased by Marshall Field Company department store in Chicago in 1904.

Craig Bates: "This is remarkable. We're talking about massive numbers of little heads on this basket. We're probably seeing two hundred bird heads. And not just acorn woodpecker heads, but bluebird heads, because with the western bluebird you have to use the head feathers to get the blue color. I think that's an important thing for us to comment on, how native arts have had to change because of the changing ecosystem in California. Largely it is the degradation of habitat for these birds that has caused their decrease in numbers."

Frank Tuttle: "It's just gorgeous. I'd like to be able to see it move, with all those pendants moving. The black would start moving when it swirls, and the pattern. Rather than being static, everything would move. Then it's doing what it's supposed to do, which is to remind us that we're in constant motion. It's not static and we're not outside of it. We're a part of it, and that's what it's doing . . . it's reminding us that we're part of a larger context."

Sherrie Smith-Ferri: "These really highly decorated, ornamented feather baskets are traditionally made by women, among the Pomo, and so they're seen as women's creations. But truthfully, all those feathers are usually gotten by the men, and the clamshell disc beads are usually made by the men. And that's a lot of work. So the basket is really a collaboration."

Mabel McKay (Pomo/Patwin) 1907–1993

GIFT BASKET
c. 1965

split sedge root (buff), willow shoots (foundation), acorn woodpecker crest (red) and chin (yellow) feathers, mallard
crest and neck feathers (green), valley quail topknot, clamshell disc beads, abalone shell
H. 1⅝" Diam. 3⅞"
Collection of Marshall McKay

Mabel Boone McKay was a sickly child who spent most of her childhood in the company of her maternal Patwin grandmother, Sarah Taylor. She recalled watching her grandmother weave, but not necessarily being taught to weave herself. By the age of twelve, Mabel had already experienced a number of powerful dreams that eventually would direct her to a life of traditional healing

Mabel McKay, 1973. Photograph by Spence Billington. Courtesy of Pacific Western Traders.

or "doctoring." She attributed her knowledge of weaving to her dreams. The spirit had provided the direction in Mabel's life and the inspiration for her basketmaking career.

Mabel was well known throughout California for her doctoring, knowledge of Pomo and Patwin traditions, fluency in the Hill Patwin language, and for her impeccable basketry. She held classes for aspiring weavers over several years. Hundreds of native and non-native people received their introduction into traditional native weaving from Mabel. For young people searching for knowledge and skills associated with the old culture, Mabel was an ever-so-important bridge. She was often requested to speak about native tradition and about her weaving at universities throughout the state.

Mabel once spoke about her feather-basketweaving tradition: "I get most of my enjoyment working with the feathers. The bird is very sacred to us. Also, the traditional weavers, when they weave their baskets, when they kill their own birds, they eat the birds. They do not let it spoil. Feather-basketweaving, we do not eat. We work couple of hours first thing in the morning. And as you get hungry, you push it to side. And when you eat, you don't touch it no more till next day." (Mabel McKay, 1974, videotaped by Dorothy Hill)

Frank LaPena: "I am always impressed by the restrictions Mabel McKay worked under. That is why I value her work: her patience and knowing there is a story to each basket."

Judith Polanich: "Mabel's feather baskets were very special to her. They're the one thing she refused to teach her students."

Craig Bates: "I remember that Mabel took this basket around with her to various demonstrations. The feather baskets that Mabel made were really in her own style. Particularly, her use of a single clamshell disc bead and abalone shell pendant in combination. That is something you don't see in older examples, which generally had a collar of clamshell disc beads at the rim just above a ruff of quail topknots. When these earlier baskets have abalone shell pendants, they are suspended by an inch or more of small glass beads, or by three or more clamshell disc beads laid side-to-side. From a survey of extant baskets in museum and private collections, it appears that the smaller-size baskets more commonly lacked the pendants. Mabel's basket differs from the earlier feathered baskets in several ways. Her abalone pendants are suspended by only one clamshell disc bead, her baskets lack the requisite collar of clamshell disc beads, and they have two rows of offset, widely spaced quail topknots, again something I've never seen in earlier baskets.

"These unique attributes of Mabel's baskets can probably be explained in several ways. Mabel always said that 'the Spirit' told her how to make baskets, so this basket may well be representative of specific instructions Mabel received. In another way, the basket can be viewed as uniquely Mabel, with her own aesthetic sense guiding its creation. The lack of a full collar of clamshell beads, three beads on the abalone pendants, and a full ruff of quail topknots may also be evidence of how clamshell disc beads were no longer readily available. I think it's important to remember that, even though Mabel was very much steeped in tradition, she was also quite an individual. And there really wasn't a circle of women around her to criticize a divergence from traditional norms in the basketry of her community like there might have been a generation or two earlier.

"And another interesting thing: if Mabel made this basket in the late 1960s, then this basket used a heck of a lot of acorn woodpecker scalps in its creation. As we all know, habitat degradation—primarily the loss of oak woodlands to development throughout central California—has resulted in a marked decrease in acorn woodpecker populations. In earlier larger feathered baskets, four or five hundred scalps would be necessary. By the 1960s it was difficult to get even forty or fifty such scalps. By then, acquisition of woodpecker feathers was illegal. Protection of the birds by federal and state laws, and the ever-present vigilance of game wardens, agents, and bird-watchers, made acquiring the feathers difficult at best. I recall that many of Mabel's friends brought her birds they found run over by automobiles. But I do wonder just how long it took Mabel to save up the forty or fifty scalps needed for this basket."

Mabel McKay (Pomo/Patwin) 1907–1993

BEADED BASKET
c. 1960

split sedge root (buff), split and dyed bulrush root (black), willow shoots (foundation), glass beads
H. 4⅜" Diam. 9⅝"
State of California, Department of Parks and Recreation

Mabel McKay's basketry was among the most sought-after Native American art in the country. When she died, there was a long list of names in the little book containing her basket waiting list. Fortunately she passed on some of her knowledge.

Here she speaks about dying the bulrush roots used in this basket: "Our black roots is the bulrush. This is a dull brown before it's dyed. Many years ago, when they dyed this bulrush, they bury it in the black mud around the creek where the black mud was. But since we don't own the land or have rights of [access], we cannot do it that way no more. So we have to do it the modern way now. So I use just a plain old pan. And I use a little acorn in it, I put some tea leaves, and I put a little dirt, and a little nail so it will rust in the water. It will take about five days. And if you overdo it, it will chip too. You got to test it just right for it to stay on." (Mabel McKay, 1974, videotaped by Dorothy Hill)

Craig Bates: "I think this is just remarkably Mabel. Nobody else in the world made baskets like this but Mabel. It's really interesting I think. Here's this woman who became a really important traditional figure later, as she got older, but in making this basket, she's made a total change, a break with tradition. Whether it was something that she dreamed or whether it was something she just decided to do, we don't know. She felt comfortable enough to do this, with these big loops of beads. It's a pretty big break for a Pomo or Patwin person before the war or even during the war. And to keep the two designs going on at the same time, one in the sedge and bulrush and another in beads, is a new idea too. Doing this kind of thing is not too common."

Judith Polanich: "But for Mabel, this makes sense. This sort of departure is very much the way she was. I was a student of hers for eight years, and I'll never forget the night she gave us a speech about 'tradition.' Mabel's view of tradition was that you dreamed the pattern. For her, tradition didn't mean that you were doing it the same way as the older generation or that you had been 'taught' by a traditional weaver."

Artist Unknown (Tubatulabal)
GIFT BASKET
c. 1905

split sedge root (buff), split devil's claw (black), dyed bracken root, (black), split and dyed bulrush root (black),
split sumac shoots (white), deer grass stalks (foundation), valley quail topknots
H. 9¼" Diam. 13½"
Peabody Museum of Archaeology and Ethnology, Harvard University

Very little is known about Tubatulabal weaving traditions. Among their coiled forms is the "bottleneck," a shape of basket also made by the Western Mono, Yokuts, Kawaiisu, and Panamint Shoshone. There is some question as to its aboriginal use, but it may have been a special basket made for gift or payment or to hold valuable articles. The design motif in this basket has a fairly wide distribution in the southern Sierra and into the Death Valley region. The Western Mono sometimes refer to this pattern as a "butterfly" motif; however, their version of the design includes only two of the small triangular projections rather than four. The vertical marks, or "ticking," on the rim are a common treatment for the rim of a Tubatulabal bottleneck basket.

Craig Bates: "On Tubatulabal baskets the butterfly designs are set off with two stitches of split shoots [white] on either side of the dark triangular motifs, instead of with sedge."

Bruce Bernstein: "This piece is so marvelous because she's chosen to highlight the design with sumac (white) which makes the bracken (black) jump out. This is such a unique use of split shoot material in California. We tend to call this design "flight of the butterfly," which may or may not be accurate, but when you are thinking about that name for this design and you look at the way she's given it dimension—that flight line—it could very well be that. It's a pretty incredible piece. You also see that she was so careful to choose her materials to get the even color. I think good weavers make it look easy."

Brian Bibby: "Are you talking about the sedge root?"

Bruce Bernstein: "All of it. All of it is so even toned. It's the grading of material, it's the tending of the places where she went to harvest those roots and sticks. The close attention she paid to those places. It's a well-tended garden. It's clear that the result of her work in harvesting and preparing her materials is that the basket has such an evenness of the hue and tone. The weaver has created a technical masterpiece, a thing of beauty."

Artist Unknown (Shoshone)
TREASURE BASKET
c. 1900

split willow shoots (buff), split devil's claw (black), porcupine quills (white)
H. 5" Diam. 6¾"
State of California, Department of Parks and Recreation

Among the Shoshone inhabiting the Panamint Range and Death Valley region of California, this form of basket may once have been used in association with cremations and/or funerals. By 1900, however, treasure baskets were largely made for sale to collectors. In this example, the weaver has incorporated the flexible white quill from the porcupine to create a brilliant contrast with the dark devil's claw sewing elements.

The design follows the form of this bottleneck basket. Each of the five evenly spaced vertical designs gradually grows in width as the diameter of the basket reaches its widest point at the shoulder; each design then narrows as the shape quickly recedes to its small opening at the neck. The border or selvage receives a different design treatment. This subtle treatment of the vertical design bands complements and emphasizes the elegant shape of the piece.

Shoshone weavers used several weaving tools. Before metal awls were available, the Panamint Shoshone used the spikes of cottontop cactus (Fowler and Dawson, 1986:720). Later Shoshone weavers punched small holes in a tin can lid and drew strands of willow or devil's claw through them to assure even-sized and especially fine sewing elements in their basketry.

Bruce Bernstein: "The first thing that draws me to this piece is its beauty, and just how carefully and meticulously it is constructed. The technical expertise needed to make this piece is a high level. The choice of materials, the choice of how well they fit together, the preparation of those materials are all flawless. The stitching is also flawless. The weaver makes a very unusual use of the quill. You sometimes find quills in baskets but they're generally little spots of color. For this weaver to choose to use quill exclusively as she would use any other sewing strand is a pretty remarkable thing—the basket stands out because of that. This is quite likely porcupine quill, however, it could also be domestic leghorn chicken quill. And this is one of those things that make baskets wonderful, that the materials are transformed by the weavers in such a way that they become difficult to identify.

"This bottleneck form, I believe, is indigenous. The evidence suggests it was used as a gift or treasure basket. A gift or treasure basket could be used at a [funeral] burning, as an offering. You also give that same kind of gift basket for payment to a doctor, or as a gift at at wedding, or to mark a person's birth. It's a payment. What we don't know is whether the shape and size of a bottleneck signifies something as well.

"The designs on much of Panamint Shoshone coiled works are often set vertically. That's because people at that particular time didn't live with furniture, but lived looking down into the containers on the ground. That's the way they saw the containers, so they wove them in such a manner to provide the best visual impact from that particular vantage point."

CONTINUITY AND CHANGE

Mrs. Graham (Chukchansi) c. 1870–c. 1930
BASKET
c. 1905

split sedge root (buff), dyed bracken root (black),
common flicker quills (pink), deer grass stalks (foundation)
H. 6½" Diam. 12"
Department of Anthropology, Smithsonian Institution

The identity of "Mrs. Graham," to whom this basket is attributed, is unclear. However, it is interesting to note that the 1910 U.S. census report included a Mary Graham and listed her occupation as "basketmaker." She was Chukchansi, a group of foothill people who are linguistically, culturally, and historically related to the many distinct communities that are often grouped under the generalized term "Yokuts." Historically, Yokuts people occupied most of the southern San Joaquin Valley and many of the adjacent eastern foothills.

In addition to making coiled works such as this, the Chukchansi made a number of twined wares used primarily for gathering and processing foods. An unusual feature of this basket is the use of red-shafted flicker quills as weft elements.

Craig Bates: "This has to be one of the most beautiful Chukchansi Yokuts baskets in existence. The striking contrast of the black bracken root with the salmon-orange of the flicker quills is unique in collections of Yokuts or any other basketry.

"While Chukchansi women have told me about people doing this sort of thing long ago, it was always, apparently, somewhat of an unusual practice. The feather quills are somewhat slick and are not an easy material to weave in a coiled basket. The basket is just marvelous."

Fannie Brown (Wintu) c. 1867–c. 1940

STORAGE BASKET

c. 1905

split conifer root (buff), bear grass (white), woodwardia fern stem dyed with alder bark (rust), maidenhair fern stem (black), willow shoots? (foundation)
H. 5½" Diam. 7"
The Oakland Museum of California

Fannie Brown lived in the upper Sacramento River drainage area of Shasta County. She was a noted shaman among her people and had a considerable reputation. Many considered her a dangerous person, with the ability to "poison." A contemporary, Sadie Marsh, once said, "Fannie is strong in poisoning, that is why people won't call her when they get sick." (Du Bois, 1935:111) Fannie Brown explained that her first experience in becoming a shaman occurred when her nephew died in her arms. Crying, she fell unconscious, and in a dream, she saw a spirit woman with tattoo marks on her face come to take the dead boy away. Among her personal shamanic paraphernalia, she wore a necklace made of rattles obtained from rattlesnakes she had killed.

Frank Tuttle: "There's an interesting visual impact, an interplay, in the separation of the light upper and lower portions of the pattern [as if they had once fit together and been pulled apart]. This break, this 'opening up,' reveals an underlying pattern contrary to the outside, overlaid pattern of color. It's visually engaging and highly effective."

Jean LaMarr: "It's very artistic."

Fannie Brown, undated. From Cora Du Bois, "Wintu Ethnography," University of California Publications in *American Archaeology and Ethnology* 36, no. 1 (1935).

Denise Davis: "It's like you're peeking into something. The artist has prepared a surprise for you with her choice of color placement in the design. She's directed your focus to one place."

Frank LaPena: "The alternating of the red and black, as a pattern within the design, is common in a lot of Wintu baskets. Also characteristic is the horizontal relationship of patterns, sometimes inside designs, as in this case."

Mary Kintano (Cahuilla) 1877–1934

CUP
1908

split dyed and undyed juncus stalks (black and field), juncus stalks (foundation)
H. 2¾" Diam. 4"
Pomona College, Claremont, California. Gift of Emil P. Steffa, 1933

Mary Kintano (often spelled Quintano) was a resident of the Torres-Martinez Reservation in Riverside County. It is probable that she was in her early thirties at the time this basket was made.

Frank LaPena: "I react to the shape and the form as a cup. But the way the design works, it really moves me into it, so that I have to react aesthetically. Because I need to see how even it is, how and what it feels like. That black design setting on there just pulls me right in. I want to feel that thing. I just feel like I've got to hold that. It's like when you see a sculpture and you want to lift it up to see if it's right."

Donna Largo: "She was a Desert Cahuilla from Torres-Martinez [Reservation]. And I've seen some other baskets of hers. This one's really nice. It's the lightning pattern."

Guadalupe Arenas (Cahuilla) c. 1880–1958

BASKET

c. 1910

split dyed and undyed juncus stalks (field and black), split sumac shoots (white), deer grass (foundation)
H. 4¾" Diam. 10¼"
The Palm Springs Desert Museum, gift of James Smeaton Chase

Guadalupe Arenas was raised near Indio and later worked in the Palm Springs area. Her basket incorporates a rattlesnake design, a motif that was quite popular among the Cahuilla and other native peoples of southern California after the turn of the century.

Donna Largo: "She was from Santa Rosa Reservation. I knew her when I was a little girl. I remember that she was quiet and that she spoke Indian, the Cahuilla language. The rattlesnake and the eagle in the basket, that is like her signature. Her baskets, basically, all had those figures in them. My grandmother told me a story about the rattlesnake and how it got into the basket. She said that the women would all sit around on the ground making baskets and a rattlesnake kept coming toward one lady. And she'd chase him away and chase him away. And he kept coming back. And finally she told the rattlesnake, 'If you don't go away, I'm going to put you in my basket.' Well, he wouldn't go away, so that's how we got rattlesnakes in our baskets."

Jean LaMarr: "Two strong life forms."

Frank LaPena: "Not only are the forms dominant because of their size, but the 'signature' symbol line [the isolated bar above the snake] fits."

L. Frank Manriquez: "People know that the snake is a strong person. [At one time it was said,] no weaver made a rattlesnake design in a basket for fear of going blind. At some point a weaver risked her sight to honor the snake. After that, others wove snake designs and no one has ever heard of a blinding."

Guadalupe Arenas (left) and Marguerita Pablo (right). Courtesy of The Southwest Museum.

Magdelena Augustine (Chemehuevi) 1877–c. 1945

BASKET
c. 1914

natural and dyed (black) juncus stalks, split sumac shoots (white)
H. 10⅝" Diam. 15⅛"
Pomona College, Claremont, California. Gift of Emil P. Steffa, 1933

The basketry of Magdelena (or Madelena) Augustine shows some differences from that of her Chemehuevi relatives living farther to the east near the Colorado River. One major difference is the use of native Cahuilla materials, such as juncus, for weft strands. Her husband was a Cahuilla, and the two lived on the Augustine Reservation near the Salton Sea in Riverside County.

L. Frank Manriquez: "I'm looking at the bottom part of the juncus plant, the red, the use of that for the interior, and the dyed juncus for the black outline. The negative space between the stitches is just as pretty to me as the design stitches."

Donna Largo: "I know that when I make baskets and use the red, I match all the darker reds and lighter reds and then start putting them in there. Juncus stalks have different colors in them. They can start off really dark red at the bottom and then get lighter toward the top, or they can be real dark all the way up. If you pick juncus too early, it's real pink. The mountain juncus is really dark red, and then toward San Diego it's more orange. I think that's because of the different elevations. Where I pick my juncus, in Cahuilla, is over a sulfur spring. So the color is completely different than in other areas. I also pick on another side of the mountain, where it's not quite as dark. I really think the sulfur water it gets has a lot to do with the color. We pull the juncus out of the ground instead of cutting it."

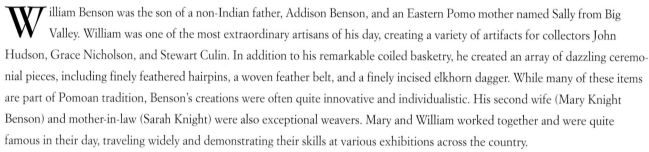

William Benson (Eastern Pomo) 1862–1937

STICK PIN WITH MINIATURE BASKET

c. 1915

split sedge root (buff), split and dyed bulrush root (black), garnet gemstone, gold
Overall length (pin and basket) 2⅛" H. (basket) ⅛" Diam. (basket) ⅜"
The Grace Hudson Museum, City of Ukiah

William Benson was the son of a non-Indian father, Addison Benson, and an Eastern Pomo mother named Sally from Big Valley. William was one of the most extraordinary artisans of his day, creating a variety of artifacts for collectors John Hudson, Grace Nicholson, and Stewart Culin. In addition to his remarkable coiled basketry, he created an array of dazzling ceremonial pieces, including finely feathered hairpins, a woven feather belt, and a finely incised elkhorn dagger. While many of these items are part of Pomoan tradition, Benson's creations were often quite innovative and individualistic. His second wife (Mary Knight Benson) and mother-in-law (Sarah Knight) were also exceptional weavers. Mary and William worked together and were quite famous in their day, traveling widely and demonstrating their skills at various exhibitions across the country.

Miniature baskets have been popular among Pomoan weavers for many years. The setting of the garnet stone in this particular piece is quite unusual, in the way that it appears to be set snugly within the basket and attached to the stick pin.

Sherrie Smith-Ferri: "A true artist and a very fine craftsman."

Frank Tuttle: "And the notion that it was somehow built around that stone in there is just amazing, almost unbelievable. Baskets have this sort of historical sense about them. When we look at baskets, we think of them as being in the past. We think

of the making of baskets as being sort of limited—technique-wise, material-wise—in order to fit into certain criteria. And then here's this beautiful pin, this obvious example of manipulation of materials and technical wizardry, and we want to attribute it to a more recent time, because we're more familiar with micro-chips and others types of small things. Given all those decades ago, it's quite a creation."

Sherrie Smith-Ferri: "It's very innovative. You get the sense that Benson probably just wanted to see if he could do it. He probably had an idea and wanted to see if it would work. A really dazzling piece."

William Benson, 1931. Photograph by Jaime de Angulo. Courtesy of Phoebe Apperson Hearst Museum of Anthropology, University of California, Berkeley.

Frank Tuttle: "Yeah, sort of a showmanship type of thing—along with the other things he did, the feather belts, that one dagger, the ear sticks. Those are very elegant, very fine. Here, the weavers [weft elements] almost take on a linear quality, almost like an etching. It's so tiny. Just a tiny manipulation of line, a physical line. That's how I see baskets anyway. But here, right off, what one sees is just the pattern. One doesn't visually take in the texture of the weave."

Sherrie Smith-Ferri: "And this is something that would be very stylish today. I would love to wear it."

Frank Tuttle: "It's timeless. It really shows how well he knows his materials and what can be done. He's extending the possibilities of the materials and the techniques. And now, in our own communities, we don't have enough of the activity occurring to determine what the possibilities are, what the limitations are. So we may be afraid to suggest what the possibilities could be, because we just haven't seen it. But here, in this little pin, we have a very elegant example of what the possibilities could be."

Elizabeth Hickox (Wiyot) 1873–1947
LIDDED TRINKET BASKET
c. 1916

Oregon grape root (interior weft), maidenhair fern stem (black), porcupine quill dyed with wolf moss (yellow), myrtle shoots (foundation)
H. 5¼" Diam. 7"
Private Collection

Elizabeth Conrad Hickox (known as Lizzie) was the daughter of a Wiyot woman and a German father. Her mother was witness to one of the worst massacres of native people in the state, in February of 1860, when approximately fifty Wiyot were killed by vigilantes on Gunther Island in Humboldt Bay. Elizabeth's parents settled at Somes Bar on the Klamath River in the heart of Karuk country, and there she was raised. Her mother, Polly Conrad Steve, was a weaver and was probably Elizabeth's primary teacher.

Elizabeth's weaving may represent some of the finest twining ever done. Her baskets—with their dramatic use of maidenhair fern (black) as a background field rather than a conservative design element, and their elegant shape, which often exhibits a concave camber to the outer wall as it restricts toward the rim—represent a mastery of technique, design, and vision that is truly virtuoso, even in a community where so many women created such outstanding work. Beginning in 1908 and extending into the 1930s

Mrs. Hickox's baskets were marketed by the premier merchant in Native American art at the time, Grace Nicholson of Pasadena. Elizabeth's baskets were collected by museums and well-to-do collectors throughout the United States.

Elizabeth developed a remarkably distinctive style of lidded baskets. In this basket, her dramatic use of two colors follows a pattern a Yurok weaver described to ethnologist Lila O'Neale in 1936. O'Neale later wrote, "A downriver cap-maker frequently visualized the [black-and-white] pictures of baskets as they might be developed in certain colors. In all her descriptions, yellow was used in smallest amount. She explained that the larger areas in a motif should be of black fern because the strong color area of quills needs the balance of dark. What she actually said was that no one would ever make a big mark of yellow quills and a little mark of black fern."

Vivien Hailstone: "Where she lived, there were lots of ferns all along the side of the hill. She had ferns galore. So, that's why she used a lot of black [maidenhair] fern."

Kathy Wallace: "Well, the challenge is getting the materials. Was she able to use them fresh, then? When they're fresh, it's easier to weave them."

Vivien Hailstone: "Yes, but they need to be dried [slightly] first."

Kathy Wallace: "Her starts were decorative. She started weaving the basket in the traditional technique, and then turned the bottom outside to the inside. Then she continued weaving: what had started as the inside undecorated part of the basket, she made into the outside overlaid part of the basket. Her designs always continued on the lid."

Brian Tripp: "I remember seeing her show on the coast, with a whole group of these baskets, some of the most perfect baskets. The technique and everything. They're just like little jewels. Exactly like jewels."

Craig Bates: "The interesting thing is how many there are of these [kinds of baskets]. I don't know exactly how many, but there are definitely more than twenty, maybe more than fifty. And they range in size from three inches to a foot."

Judith Polanich: "If we're focusing on baskets as art, this basket makes a nice statement. I mean, this form is modeled on a

storage basket: it has a lid and you put things in it to keep them safe. Yet, if you open this basket, you find that the storage idea is completely negated by the design. There is a design on the inside, but it only shows on the inside, so it can only be seen when the basket is empty. So that aspect of the basket works artistically only when it's empty. If you put something into the basket, activating the storage function, you are taking something away from it artistically."

L. Frank Manriquez: "As an artist, I don't see where her problems were. There were no problems to overcome, no solutions. There was just making things. I don't know that these baskets challenged her. They look so perfect."

Craig Bates: "I think her success is making them look that way."

Brian Tripp: "If you were to look at all of her stuff, you'd see where she'd take the designs and do just one more step that made them incredible."

Elizabeth Hickox, undated. Courtesy of The Huntington Library.

Carrie Bethel (Paiute) 1898–1974

BASKET
1929

split sedge root (buff), dyed bracken root (black), split winter redbud shoots (reddish), willow shoots (foundation)
H. 3⅛" Diam. 6⅛"
The Yosemite Museum, National Park Service

Born Carrie McGowan near Mono Lake at the edge of the eastern Sierra, she finished her first basket when she was ten. By the 1920s she was an accomplished weaver and a prominent competitor in the Yosemite and June Lake Indian Field Days. During this period many of her finest works were purchased by wealthy San Francisco collector James Schwabacher. In 1939 Carrie gave demonstrations of weaving at the Indian Exhibition of the Golden Gate International Exposition held on Treasure Island. She was adept at a number of basketmaking techniques. In addition to the traditional twining methods used by Paiute weavers to produce most of their utilitarian pieces, she produced over a hundred single-rod beaded baskets. (Bates, 1995) But it is her three-rod coiled baskets with their striking polychromatic design motifs that made her famous. They represent her most demanding and finest works.

Craig Bates: "Carrie Bethel was probably one of the most innovative weavers in the Yosemite-Mono Lake region. She was about thirty when she wove this basket. When she started weaving, she began making all these new patterns that nobody had made before. Baskets made this way, with these materials, weren't made before 1900. They start to be made around 1908 and are well developed by 1912. At the end of the 1920s Carrie Bethel is making numbers of baskets in this style. She just kept evolving and changing patterns. Her technology and the quality of her weaving is always extremely consistent."

Carrie Bethel, c. 1929. Courtesy of Yosemite National Park.

Carrie Bethel (Paiute) 1898–1974

BASKET
1933

split sedge root (buff), dyed bracken root (black), split winter redbud shoots (reddish), willow shoots (foundation)
H. 14" Diam. 27"
Private Collection

Carrie Bethel's weaving evolved, but the level of her skill remained constant, with the high quality of the weaving visible in pieces she made in the 1920s matched by those she produced in the 1960s.

This piece is among Carrie's largest works (the largest being more than thirty inches in diameter). The treatment of the three rows of triangles on this basket attests to Carrie's dedication to her artistry. Each of the more than one thousand slender, elongated triangles has a single weft outline. Triangles in the top and bottom rows are executed in split winter redbud shoots and outlined in black-dyed bracken root. Middle-row triangles reverse that color scheme. Switching materials for a single width stitch—a laborious task that had to be repeated many times for a basket this size—shows a remarkable dedication. And to good effect: the outlining adds a significant dimension to the overall design.

Craig Bates: "She was weaving this basket while working in the laundry at Tioga Lodge at Mono Lake in 1933. She finished it in 1933 in the summer. She's just so good. In the same decade, the 1930s, she made at least two others that are almost the same size. It would take her about three years to complete one, besides working in the laundry and weaving lots of small baskets."

L. Frank Manriquez: "Artistically, it's maniacal."

Craig Bates: "The pattern is so complex and made up of so many small elements that in some places you'd have to change materials every stitch or two. That's more splicing than I'd ever want to do."

Lena Dick (Washoe) c. 1889–1965

BASKET
c. 1934

split willow shoots (white), split winter redbud shoots (reddish), dyed bracken root (black), willow shoots (foundation)
H. 9¼" Diam. 13"
Private Collection

Lena Frank Dick was one of the premier Washoe weavers of her generation. Her fancy three-rod coiled gift baskets were reminiscent of the works of Datsolalee, who had developed and popularized this style of basket, termed *degikup* by the Washoe, a generation earlier. Indeed, several of Lena's earlier baskets were sold through Abe Cohen's Emporium at Lake Tahoe, also outlet for Datsolalee's work. And like Datsolalee, Lena Dick had a patron in Carson Valley rancher Fred Stettlemeyer, who commissioned baskets from her for Roscoe A. Day, a San Francisco orthodontist.

Lena Dick made this basket in what her biographer Dr. Marvin Cohodas describes as her most outstanding phase of work (c. 1926–1934), when her technique and artistry were at their peak. During this period her baskets were generally larger and the weaving finer, reaching thirty-three weft strands per linear inch.

Craig Bates: "The willow sewing strands are very white for a Washoe basket this old. Usually the willow will have aged to a light brown."

Judith Polanich: "I'm always interested in patterns like this, with designs that seem like beadwork, with stretched-out lines linking them. They remind me of the African Makonde sculpture, which is very attenuated and has a really strange feeling to it. The Makonde is also art created for a market, so there's another connection."

Brian Tripp: "I like it because it's not overcrowded. So you get such a beautiful background. I see the white as the background, and the black and the other stuff is just sort of laying on top. Just sort of floating."

Lena Dick, c. 1930. Courtesy of Marvin Cohodas from the collection of M. Flores.

"There's been a whole long line of people making baskets. And for an artist to step out, away from that pack, and be recognized, he or she is going to have to come up with something a little bit different—we're different people, we grow up with different sensibilities, in different times—and this basket probably filled the bill."

Craig Bates: "This basket, like the Mono Lake Paiute baskets woven by Carrie Bethel, isn't from an old tradition. This type of basket is a new invention. People didn't make baskets in this form before, so the weavers didn't have to follow any tradition. So they were free to experiment, like you say, free to break out and try new things."

Kathy Wallace: "I like it because it leaves a lot of exposed coils, so you're looking at the fine work that was put into the basket, not just the design."

Mary Wrinkle (Shoshone) 1876–1940

BASKET
c. 1939

split willow shoots (white), split juncus stalks (yellow-orange), split and dyed bulrush root (black),
Joshua tree root (reddish), willow shoots (foundation)
H. 3½" Diam. 6¾"
Collection of Eva Slater

Mary Wrinkle is still remembered throughout the Owens Valley, not just for her basketry, but for her outgoing personality and good humor. Originally from the arid Saline Valley, north of Death Valley, Mary later married and moved to Keeler on the shores of Owens Lake (now dry), where she and her husband worked for the Soda Works plant. It was from the plant manager that her husband Charlie took the surname Wrinkle. In about 1910 the Wrinkles moved to the mining town of Darwin.

Around this time, and in a new setting, Mary apparently set aside old basketmaking traditions and created new forms and images. At first she continued to use the two-color scheme in the old Shoshone style and with great precision, often achieving over fifty stitches per linear inch. Over the years Mary included additional colors and materials in her work, among them the yellow from juncus rush, red from the yucca tree root, a bright white from porcupine quills, and, by 1930, the orange-pink of the common flicker quill.

Many of her new materials are from the sandy hills around Darwin, for example, the root of the yucca tree, which grows there at higher elevations. These trees not only provide weavers with a red basket material, but also offer nesting places and perches for the black-and-yellow Scott oriole, the subject of Mary Wrinkle's bird baskets of the 1930s. These baskets became very popular with collectors. (Slater, n.d.)

Craig Bates: "You often see birds represented in baskets, but you seldom see birds that are so real-looking. This is remarkable."

Brian Bibby: "Her exceptionally fine weaving and technique allowed her to represent these birds and plants so well that their species can be easily identified."

L. Frank Manriquez: "This is beautiful. It's so alive."

Nettie McKinnon (Karuk/Yurok) 1898–1987
PLAQUE
c. 1955

willow root (buff), bear grass (white), woodwardia fern stem dyed with alder bark (rust), maidenhair fern stem (black), willow shoots (foundation)
H. 2½" Diam. 11½"
Collection of Vivien Hailstone

Nettie Cooper McKinnon was born and raised near Bluff Creek on the Klamath River. She was a versatile weaver capable of making several different types of traditional baskets, as well such new forms as the wall plaque. Wall plaques appear to have been an invention of Klamath River weavers, who started producing them sometime after World War II. It is evidence of the ingenuity and adaptability of weavers that they were able to develop new basket forms that would appeal primarily to non-Indian customers and that could be made fairly quickly with a smaller investment of time than is often required for larger or more demanding traditional forms.

Judith Polanich: "A basket like this really shows how important innovation can be in keeping the tradition going. To take the best part of the tradition—the fine weave and the brilliant colors—and to generate new forms that younger weavers can master, and can finish in a reasonable time, helps to keep the tradition alive. This kind of innovation is such an important development.

Vivien [Hailstone] has been able to do it at Hoopa, too. Encouraging the younger women keeps basketry going in the various communities across California; and what does it is finding ways they can get to the heart of the tradition, have a finished product, and experience the excitement of that accomplishment."

Brian Tripp: "It doesn't only inspire the women; it inspires the guys too."

Kathy Wallace: "This is one of the most striking plaques I have ever seen. It's so eye-catching, even from across the room, even when it's displayed among other baskets. Nettie's starts are very distinctive, and this basket shows off the start, which is usually relegated to the bottom of the basket, and seldom seen. Her use of color or contrast in the design is what makes it stand out."

Nettie McKinnon, c. 1980s. Photograph by Larry Dalrymple.

Boquita Wilson (Atsugewi) 1888-1968
BASKET
c. 1958

split conifer root (interior weft), bear grass (white), maidenhair fern stem (black), split winter redbud shoots (reddish), willow shoots (foundation)
H. 5" Diam. 8¼"
The Redding Museum of Art and History

The Atsugewi homeland encompasses most of the Hat Creek drainage north of Mount Lassen. Atsugewi weavers call the central design element running through this piece the "lizard's foot." It is interesting to note the similarity of this piece to the next basket, which was made by Selena LaMarr, Boquita's sister.

Jean LaMarr: "What I like about this basket is that it takes the white part and makes it very important. There's a strong element of the white, which emphasizes the dark. Sometimes the white becomes the negative, or nothing, and that's very beautiful."

Kathy Wallace: "The work in this basket is extremely even and smooth for a full twist overlay twined basket."

Selena LaMarr (Atsugewi) 1892–1968
BASKET
1960

split conifer root (interior weft), maidenhair fern stem (black), bear grass (white),
split winter redbud shoots (reddish), willow shoots (foundation)
H. 6" Diam. 9"
Lassen Volcanic National Park, National Park Service

As a youth Selena Taylor LaMarr often made a summer trip with her family, from their homes on Hat Creek to the high mountains and meadows that became Lassen National Park. Here her father and uncles hunted deer, and Selena and the other women fished for trout, dug for various bulbs, and gathered manzanita berries. In 1951 Selena began performing interpretive demonstrations of various traditional Atsugewi arts for the National Park Service at Lassen, a role she fulfilled until her death.

In an interview (c. 1960) Selena recalled her first experience at gathering bear grass, the principle overlay material in Atsugewi basketry:

"We call it *mahow*. You got to gather that just about week after Fourth of July. If you gather it before, when you twist it, it's brittle, it will break. And when you gather it late, they get old just like hay. They get stiff, you can't use it.

"I went with two ladies. They had a car. We went over here to Greenville. We drove right up to it. She said, 'Well, here's the grass.' The lady said, 'Start in and pick. They grow in big bunches here among the timber and bushes.' I picked out the biggest bunch and I sit down and pull. It's kinda hard pullin', you got to watch out, you'll cut your finger. They're sharp. I sat there and pick, and I look back at these two ladies, just walkin' around. Look like they weren't pickin' any. Well, they just lookin' for the best, I thought. I sat there and pull. Pretty soon one lady come back and she says, 'That grass you're pickin's no good.' I said, '(Isn't) that grass?' She said, 'Yes, but you can't use it.' And she said, 'You ever pick before?' I said, 'No, this is my first time.' She told me, 'Come here, let me show you how to pick.' So I got up and went with her."

Frank LaPena: "These little elements at the top of the design are really interesting."

Jean LaMarr: "I think that was her trademark. It is a good example of an Atsugewi design."

Frank LaPena: "What I like about this piece is the evenness of the design within the space. The proportion. What helps balance the overall design is the three little elements at the top of the pattern. If you were to eliminate those little elements, the whole pattern would drop. . . it would sink. It's almost like the whole design is suspended. The dark, solid triangular area of black in this pattern stabilizes the whole design. It's a real nice combination, the design elements and filling a space."

Selena LaMarr, 1960. Courtesy of National Park Service, Lassen National Park. [Note that the unfinished basket at the far right is the one featured in this publication.]

Laura Somersal (Wappo/Pomo) 1892–1990

BASKET (above right)
c. 1975

split sedge root (buff), dyed bulrush root (black), willow shoots (foundation)
H. 2⅜" Diam. 4½"
Collection of The Smith Family

Laura Fish Somersal was born on the Stone Ranch near Geyserville where her father was employed. As a child, her first home was a brush-covered dwelling. She was fourteen years old before her family moved into a cabin with a floor. She spoke the Dry Creek dialect of Pomo, and was perhaps the last fluent speaker of the Wappo language. In addition to Dry Creek Pomo and Wappo, Laura knew several other native dialects and was fluent in English and proficient in Spanish. She attended neither public nor government boarding schools. As a youth she worked in the fields, picking hops and various fruit crops, and later worked as a domestic at various ranch houses.

Laura began weaving at about age nine, when a cousin, Jack Woho, handed her a coiled basket start, or "button," and encouraged her to finish it. Later, her sister-in-law Rosie taught her to gather and process materials. Laura became a master at nearly all Wappo and Pomo weaving techniques, including single- and three-rod coiling, plain, three-strand, wrapped and lattice twining, and wickerwork. As a teacher, Laura was an important link to a whole generation of weavers, native and non-native, who became interested in native basketmaking during the 1970s and 1980s. As a tribal scholar, she was a major consultant for several publications regarding Wappo and Pomoan culture and language. In 1978 Laura was honored with the first Women of Achievement Award presented by the Sonoma County Commission on the Status of Women, and a photograph of her hands at work on a basket appeared on the 1983 National Women's History Week poster. (Ortiz, 1990/91:4-5 and 1994)

In a 1991 interview with Beverly R. Ortiz, Kathleen Smith, a Dry Creek Pomo, said about her: "I remember being out in the sedge beds with Laura before the Warm Springs Dam was built. We went way up on the Dry Creek side and when we sat there at lunchtime she would say a little prayer. She didn't make a big deal out of it, she just said 'Thank you.' She said, '*yah we.*' And she pulled a little piece of her bread off of her sandwich and threw it in the plants. She said, 'Oh, I would just love to sing.'" (Ortiz,

1991/92:19) In another interview the same year with David Ludwig, Kathleen said: "She was just the consummate teacher. She was just a master artist. And . . . she just had this wonderful wry sense of humor. She was just a great person. Never stuck in an old lady role. She was very contemporary." (Ortiz, 1994)

"[W]hat put her in front of other women was the fact that she was so good at doing the baskets," remarked Bette Holmes, another Dry Creek Pomo, during an interview with Beverly R. Ortiz. "And it's something that she did when it wasn't popular. Way back when I was a little girl she was making these baskets, and she always made them for every new baby in the family . . . it was just in her, that she could no more stop making the baskets than she could stop eating, because it was just part of [her] life . . . I think what made her seem so modern and up-to-date was that she never traded anything for her Indianness. She was a Pomo, and basketry was just a part of what she always did and would always do and share with others."

Frank Tuttle: "There are a lot of things going on. It's one of those baskets that just feels very nice. That zigzag design, there are four elements, the same motif that's repeated four times, very evenly spaced around the basket. I like that because it causes this flipping, there's a visual tension. You flip from a positive design to a negative design, with those parallelograms in the inner spaces there. And there seems to be a real even tension between those parallelograms and the positive design. And there seems to be just the right amount of weight, visual weight, in there. Something I really enjoy about this basket is the strong horizontal bars on the zigzag. They add a lot of validation to the parallelograms as inner spaces, and they fit just right in the back and forth, shooting your eye back and sending it forward again, back and forth in this nice zigzag."

Sherrie Smith-Ferri: "I've always liked it. I think it's a much more successful basket because of the black finishing row. I think it would look incomplete if she hadn't done that. Somehow the black row contains it."

Frank Tuttle: "Yeah, the dark finishing row actually confines the upward movement of the zigzag pattern. It doesn't matter on the bottom because the seat of the basket is smaller than the opening at the top. So the way it sets . . . . it sets just right. It's deceptive in its simplicity, its comfortableness. It doesn't have a lot of fancy things going on, but what makes it work is the fine degree of balance between black and white, and the strong horizontal lines and the broken diagonals and the restful parallelograms, which are so nice and blank."

Laura Somersal, c. 1982. Photograph by Scott Patterson. Courtesy of Victoria Patterson.

Laura Somersal (Wappo/Pomo) 1894–1992
MINIATURE BASKET (page 105)
c. 1977

split sedge root (buff), split and dyed bulrush root (black)
H. ¾" Diam. 1½"
Collection of The Smith Family

J udith Polanich: "Laura could do everything. She made meticulous miniature baskets like this, hundreds of them, each just perfectly made. She made feather baskets, too. I was with her one Sunday afternoon when a family of Mexican farm workers brought her two dried pheasant pelts. They had heard that she could make feather baskets. Once she made a feather basket from a parakeet that had died. The children wanted her to "save" their pet for them. And Laura could do fine Pomo close twining. I never thought I'd have a chance to learn, but she got me started on a mush boiler. But when I think about Laura, it's not her weaving that I remember, it's her self. She was such a lovely person. So gracious. When that family brought her the pheasant, they were dressed for a state occasion, the kids all freshly combed and in their best. She thanked them in Spanish and spent time talking to them about her baskets. I'm sure they'll never forget that afternoon. She was like that with everyone."

Sherrie Smith-Ferri: "This little one-stick basket, it's a very different basket if you look at the pattern on the bottom, a sort of flower design, or star design, than if you look at it from the side. That pattern almost disappears unless you flip it upside down. You wouldn't know it was there."

Frank Tuttle: "Yes, that's true. There's another basket I'm thinking about that has this same sort of large, wide diamond. The wide part of the diamond occurs on the bulge of the basket, and then with this small one here, see how it thins again? So you get this kind of billowing. Your eye spreads out with the wide diamond, and then it moves back in with these small black vertical diamonds. And it just moves in and out like that."

Sherrie Smith-Ferri: "And actually, if you look at the top row, it ends up being a very neat checkerboard. This little one was given to us at our wedding by my grandma. My grandfather bought a lot of Laura's little miniature baskets. He really liked her work and she liked to weave for him. I think it's kind of illustrative of the use of baskets by native families today still to mark important events in different ways. And, in fact, a lot of the weaving that's going on today is being done for native people by native people."

Frank Tuttle: "For native reasons. Which is real important for me as a native person. And also for me as an artist, because oftentimes as I think of my pieces, my making of things has to do with who it's for. When we look at baskets and look at ourselves, review ourselves as Indian people and see ourselves strung out with the history, we have to remember that a lot of things have happened to us without our consent, and with our consent. And a large part of why we have survived is because of our consent. We've said to ourselves, we want to do that, and baskets have been a real visible part of saying this part of us is very important. And it may have diminished in its activity in our communities, but its intent hasn't. Because it's still very important."

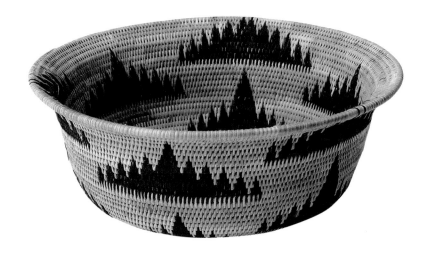

Myrtle McKay Chavez (Pomo/Wintu) 1939–

BASKET
c. 1979

split sedge root (buff), split and dyed bulrush root (black), willow shoots (foundation)
H. 2⅞" Diam. 8"
U.S. Army Corps of Engineers, Sacramento District

Myrtle McKay Chavez was born on the Big Valley Rancheria in Lake County, but has lived in the Santa Rosa area most of her life. It was not until 1971, when she was in her mid-thirties, that she began to weave, with instruction from her mother's aunt, master weaver Laura Somersal. As Myrtle recalled in a 1993 interview with Dot Brovarney, "There was a neighbor of mine who wanted to go to basket classes, which I didn't want to go to. I knew that Auntie started teaching, but I didn't want to go. I didn't think I wanted to learn baskets. Then my neighbor convinced me that it was relaxation, so I went with her. I learned to weave the baskets and she didn't." Myrtle's memories of that period reveal that her teacher had a traditional insistence on quality, thoroughness, and discipline: "I don't know how many times she made me rip the basket out and go around again. She made sure I learned right. She showed me what my mistake was and told me what I had to do. Sometimes I'd be in a hurry and I'd put two stitches in one, and she'd tell me to take it out. Or I didn't connect the rod right or something and have to take it out. She was a good teacher."

Myrtle makes both three-rod and single-rod coiled baskets. As design material, she prefers the black-dyed bulrush root, which she gathers in November and December. Myrtle also weaves feather baskets, having learned the difficult technique from the late Pomo weaver, Elsie Allen.

Judith Polanich: "Part of what you're seeing in this basket is the technique. Single-rod will always give you this comb-edge patterning. That's part of what it is. The two colors interlock with each other, and so you don't get a hard edge."

Sherrie Smith-Ferri: "Another part of the technique you see in this basket is the smooth surface of the basket walls. Single-rod baskets are always smooth, not like the corrugated walls of three-rod baskets."

Myrtle McKay Chavez (right) with her aunt, Laura Somersal, c. 1980. Photograph by Scott Patterson. Courtesy of Victoria Patterson.

Leroy Fisher (Chemehuevi) c. 1954–

TRAY
1990

split willow shoots (white), split devil's claw (black), split juncus stalks (orange), whole willow shoots (foundation)
H. 2¼" Diam. 8¾"
Collection of Larry Dalrymple

Leroy Fisher is a very active weaver living along the Colorado River on the California-Arizona border. He began weaving in the mid-1970s under the instruction of Chemehuevi master weaver Mary Lou Brown. The snake figure depicted on the basket is a Mohave rattlesnake. Leroy stated that his grandmother, Kate Fisher, had used the design in her baskets. On occasion he has seen these snakes coiled under an old mesquite tree near the spot where he weaves. (Dalrymple, 1995)

L. Frank Manriquez: "Leroy's workmanship is tight and strong. This design is immediate and lasting."

Frank LaPena: "This is a solid, regimented design. Everything seems to be even. It's bold."

Leroy Fisher, c. 1988. Photograph by Larry Dalrymple.

COILING

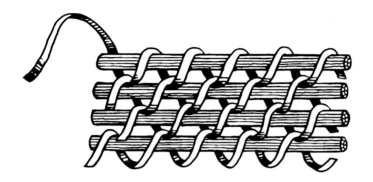

Grass bundle (interlocking stitch)   side view

Single-rod (interlocking stitch)   side view

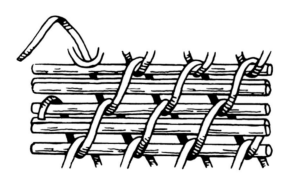

Three-rod (interlocking stitch)   side view

TWINING

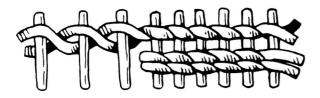

Plain twining pitch down to right

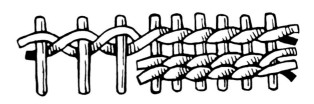

Plain twining pitch up to right

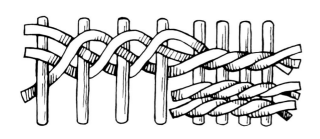

Three-strand twining

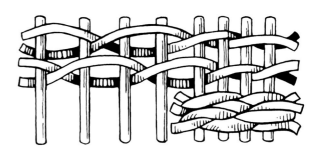

Diagonal twining

Lattice twining

BIBLIOGRAPHY

Bates, Craig D. Personal Communication. 1995.

Bates, Craig D. and Brian Bibby. "Amanda Wilson: Maidu Weaver." In *American Indian Art Magazine,* Volume 9, Number 3, 1984, pp. 38–43.

Bates, Craig D. and Martha J. Lee, *Tradition and Innovation: A Basket History of the Indians of the Yosemite-Mono Lake Area.* Yosemite National Park: The Yosemite Association, 1990.

Bernstein, Bruce. *Native American Basketry: The Hartman Collection*. Saint Joseph, MO.: The Albrecht Kemper Museum of Art, 1996.

Blackburn, Thomas C. and Kat Anderson (editors). *Before the Wilderness: Environmental Management by Native Californians.* Menlo Park: Ballena Press, 1993.

Brovarney, Dot. Interview with Myrtle McKay Chavez, February 26, 1993. Unpublished.

Busch, Briton Cooper. *Alta California, 1840–1842: The Journal and Observations of William Dane Phelps, Master of the Ship* Alert. Glendale: The Arthur H. Clarke Company, 1983.

Coues, Elliott. *On the Trail of a Spanish Pioneer: The Diary and Itinerary of Francisco Garces in His Travels through Sonora, Arizona, and California, 1775–1776.* New York: Francis P. Harper, 1900.

Culin, Stewart. Report on the Collecting Expedition among the Indians of New Mexico and California, May 4–September 29, 1907. Unpublished manuscript. The Brooklyn Museum.

Dalrymple, Larry. 1995. Personal Communication.

Du Bois, Cora. "Wintu Ethnography." In *University of California Publications in American Archaeology and Ethnology,* Volume 36, Number 1, 1935.

Fowler, Catherine S. and Lawrence E. Dawson. "Ethnographic Basketry." In *Handbook of North American Indians*, Volume 11: Great Basin. Warren L. D'Azevedo, volume editor. Washington, D.C.: Smithsonian Institution, 1986.

Hill, Dorothy. Videotape footage of weavers Mabel McKay and Bertha (Wright) Mitchell at Chico State College, 1974.

Kelsey, Andrea. "Interview with Ada Charles." In *I Am These People.* Exhibition catalogue. Governor's Office, State Capitol, Sacramento. 1975.

Liljeblad, Sven and Catherine S. Fowler. "The Owens Valley Paiute." *In Handbook of North American Indians*, Volume 1, Great Basin. Warren L. D'Azevedo, volume editor. Washington, D.C.: Smithsonian Institution, 1986.

McLendon, Sally and Brenda Holland. "The Basketmaker. The Pomoans of California." In *The Ancestors. Native Americans of the Americas.* Anna C. Roosevelt and James G.E. Smith, editors. New York: Museum of the American Indian, 1979.

Mendelsohn, Pam. "Northwest California Basketry." In *Southwest Art*, June 1983, pp. 59–60.

O'Neale, Lila M. "Yurok-Karok Basketweavers." In *University of California Publications in American Archaeology and Ethnology* Volume 32, Number 1, 1932.

Ortiz, Beverly R. "California Indian Basketweavers Gathering: A Special Report." In *News from Native California,* Volume 6, Number 1, 1991/92, pp. 13–36.

——— "With Respect: Laura Fish Somersal, 1892–1990." *News from Native California,* Volume 5, Number 1, 1990/91, pp. 4–5.

———*Pomo Basketweavers: A Tribute to Three Elders.* Video. Cotati: Creative Light Productions, 1994.

Slater, Eva. Unpublished manuscript on Panamint Shoshone basketry.

Smith, Lori. Personal Communication. 1995.

Zigmond, Maurice. "Kawaiisu Basketry." In *The Journal of California Anthropology,* Volume 5, Number 2, 1978, pp. 199–215.